Soul Refining

Inspirational Psychology for Self-Ecology!

Soul-Refining is in Self-Redefining!

Rimaletta Ray, Ph.D.

ISBN: 978-1-64999-016-7   (Paperback Edition)
ISBN: 978-1-64999-017-4   (Hardcover Edition)
ISBN: 978-1-64999-015-0   (E-book Edition)

Book Ordering Information

Phone Number: 347-901-4929 or 347-901-4920
Email: info@globalsummithouse.com
Global Summit House
www.globalsummithouse.com

Printed in the United States of America

Dedication

I dedicate this book to any

lost, abused, or broken soul!

It's never too late

to become back whole!

To Be Soul-Refining

<u>Keep Dreaming and Becoming!</u>

It's the time to cut the Godardian Knot -

our mortal and divine duality.

<u>What is What?</u>

<u>Don't Be Soul-Negligent; Be Soul-Intelligent!</u>

Preface

Let's Commit to Being Soul-Fit!

*The world is suffocating from hate, religious blindness, racism, nationalism, fascism, limited worldview, dark, undeveloped intelligence, and the minds, indoctrinated with anti-Semitism, anti-Muslimism, anti-black people **shallow self-consciousness**.*

*Our souls are conflicted between the desire to get and the imbued wish to give. The self-destructive emotions channel our lives and **the immediate gratification whims** destroy our souls' dreams.*

"We have mis-wired the circuitry of spiritual electricity in our souls!"

(Nicola Tesla)

The question is how to educate and raise a person to justify his / her unique mission on Earth?

How can we help ourselves?

"Humanity is at once the glory and the shame

of the universe, and we are responsible for both!"

(Rav. P. S. Berg)

We're Moving Onward, Upward, and Godward!

What is your Direction Toward?

To Become a Holy Luminary Inside, Charge Your Soul's Might!

Solarize Your Soul

with Intelligence,

Kindness, and

Self-Control!

- - - - - - - - - - -

Change Completely:

From Head to Toe-

From the Body to the Soul -

Become Spiritually Whole!

- -

The Fractals of Intellectually Spiritualized Beings:

Form   +   *Content*

(Body+ Spirit+ Mind) + (Self-Consciousness + Universal Consciousness)

= A new Intellectually Spiritualized You!

*(See the first book **"I'm Free to Be the Best of Me!"**- physical dimension)*

Live Consciously and Without a Frown;

Slow Up Your Slow Down!

We Are All Just Human Clay!

We are all just human clay

That God sculptures in His own way!

> *He uplifts each of us*
>
> *From the common animal ass!*

As the Phoenix bird,

We can rise from the ashes with His word!

> *But we falter along the way,*
>
> *We resist the sculptor's hand - we decay!*

We prostitute ourselves for money

Sex, treachery, cruelty and wine!

> *The Monetary God*
>
> *Is presiding the world!*

He has the satanic power

To personally devour

> *Each one of us*
>
> *And the entire human mass!*

Christ's consciousness has yet to surface

Upon every one's soul's face.

> --------------------
>
> *We need to surpass*
>
> *Ourselves in a mass*

By the morals that are celestial,

Not overly terrestrial!

For being integral, sincere, and kind

Can reside only in a super-human mind!

Since time and space are in the progression

Of a great cosmic compression,

We have no time to regress

There's only one way - to progress!

So, go beyond a mere survival

<u>And be One with the Word of the Torah, Koran or the Bible!</u>

Wage a self-limitation War –

Rule your life by "Less is More!"

Also, Zip your Soul!

It must be hermetically sealed to be preserved and

Goodness instilled in its human surf!

----

*"Everyone of us has a soul, and that soul is clearly aware
that it has a spiritual agenda."* (Michel Newton)

Auto-Induction:

I'm working on My Soul's Holistic Reformation

<u>**Now! WOW!!!**</u>

To Be a Spiritual Guru,

Tap into a Pure Spiritual Current in you!

Halleluiah to Our Spiritual Stem from the
Time of Eden!

Table of Contents

The Main Parts of the Book in Its Conceptual Nook

Five Stages of Soul-Refining   pp. 88 - 93

(Physical, Emotional, Mental, Spiritual, Universal Dimensions of Soul-Reformation)

1. Live Today Without Any Dismay!
2. The Manual of Life is the Soul's Magic Wand!
3. The Evolution of the Soul
4. Put Your Soul Refining into the Evolutionary Perspective of Redesigning

The Physical Dimension of Soul-Resurrection

1. *The Soul's Health is My Main Wealth!*
2. *I Am a Homo Sapience! (An Inspirational Booster)*
3. *The Evolution of the Soul (An Inspirational Booster)*
4. *Step One- Create Order in Yourself!*
5. *Self-Destruction is Evil -Not Civil!*
6. *Tame yourself in Every Life Realm!*
7. *Connect the Mind and the Heart - Be Smart!*
8. *Self-Discipline is on the Scene!*
9. *Clean Your Inner Chaos!*
10. *Observe Your Soul's Hygiene!*
11. *My New life Paradigm! (An Inspirational Booster)*

Stage Two - Emotional Diplomacy vs. the Soul's Obstinacy! (*Self-Monitoring*)

1. *The Soul's Trajectory of Love*
2. *Our Present-Day Emotional-Mental State*
3. *Self-Monitor Your Emotional Phone;*
4. *To Soul-Rewind, Be Kind to the Unkind!*
5. *The Trajectory of True Love*
6. *The Choices we Make dictate the Life We Live!*
7. *Love Normalcy is the Product of Intelligence and Emotional Diplomacy!*
8. **Auto-Suggestive Inspirational Hygiene is on the Scene!**
9. *The State of Love (An Inspirational Booster)*
10. *Stop the Ruling of Lust at Last! (An Inspirational Booster)*
11. *Be in a Hurry to Understand! (An Inspirational Booster)*
12. *Let's Create the Space of Love! (An Inspirational Booster)*
13. *My Happy Love Portion is Love and Devotion! (An Inspirational Booster)*
14. *Preserve Your Inner Symphony's Surf! (An Inspirational Booster)*
15. *Our Unification in Love is the Soul's Stuff! (An Inspirational Booster)*
16. *The One that is Godless is Loveless!*

Stage Three – Soul's *Discovery* (*Self-Installation*)

1. *Step Three- I Am Free to Be the Best of Me!*
2. *Not to Ever Despair, Be More Life-Aware!*
3. *The Blueprint of the Mental Soul Enrichment*
4. *Disconnected Souls are Prone to Become Foes!*
5. *Mind + Heart Unity Beats Self-Perpetuity!*
6. *The Art of Being is the Art of Becoming!*
7. *The Art of Thinking is Souls Linking!*
8. *Auto-Suggestive Inspirational Hygiene Needs to Be on the Scene!*
9. *Intelligence or Ego (An Inspirational Booster)*
10. *"Language is the Skin of Your Soul!"*
11. *Become Intellectual Aristocracy (An Inspirational Booster)*

6. I Run My Own Soul!
7. I'm a Woman / Man Ispolin!
8. I Channel My Thought by the Almighty God!
9. I Infuse My Self-Realization Fuse!
10. In My Thought, I Live Upward!

1. My Final Soul's Declaration for Inner Elation
2. The Soul's Ammunition is in Mission!

"We can never make our souls more noble unless we learn to recognize the good things done by people first and minimize their mistakes next. Learning to live with dignity is the hardest job we have."

(Anton Chekov)

Change Means Mind-Refilling and Character-Building!

Let's apply science + technology to our new life's strategy!

Science is the contemporary language of life, taking us beyond the boundaries of our survival to

the universal life's revival!

www.language-fitness.com / Check out the video / section Self-Resurrection)

Strategize Your Life and Channel it Holistically to Thrive!

I Can Embrace the Whole with My Soul!

The Philosophy of Soul-Refinement Can be Fortified by the Digital Incitement!

Create Yourself in the Life-Web Cell!

(The second book in the paradigm of Self-Creation - Emotional dimension

(Check out the first book on Self-Resurrection "I'm Free to Be the Best of Me!" – physical dimension)

The Auto-Suggestive Methodology for Soul Ecology

Self-Applied Psycho-Culture can fix any Soul's Fracture!

Strengthen Your Personal Gene with the Mind-Inductive Hygiene!

15

1. The Inspirational Psychology for the Soul's Ecology

In my five books, on Self-Resurrection, featuring five levels of self-creation, (*physical, emotional, mental, spiritual, and universal*) of which this book presents the emotional dimension of life, I am continuously writing about the most beneficial effect of the Auto -Suggestive Psychology for Self-Ecology

I love the inspirational message of the book, "*Superjoy*" by *Dr. Paul Pearsall*. I found it lying on the ground among many other old, dirty books that were being sold by a street seller in Manhattan on the third day of my immigration to the USA from Latvia. In the turmoil of my life then, the title of the book that caught my eye and the book itself became the ray of hope for me till this day. That's the psychology that I follow in my auto-suggestive messages.

"Joy-ology" is my Psychology!

So, I suggest inducting your mind with *the rhyming inspirational* and *psychologically charged boosters* and *mind-sets* (*authoritative commands to the mind here.*) because "the rhyming word gets better inward" and it easier comes to the mind when it's most needed to boost the spirit and add some emotional gas to a sagging psyche. We need books that inspire and help the tension to rewire!

Books should be like works of Art, easy to digest and colorfully smart!

To change yourself, you need to **AUTHORITATIVELY CHANGE YOUR THINKING** or "*do the reprogramming of your cells*" *(Dr. Bruce Lipton)*, your minicomputers that are at your service *to enhance your connection to the Universal Intelligence* through your own AUTO-MEDIA - your aware attention to life and living. You need to tune it up to the messages from the Above that you get thanks to your INTUITION – your direct line to God.

Thus, you will become a true master of your subconscious mind that will follow your conscious commands and channel you on the path of your soul's *Self-Resurrection* in the right direction with an uplifted spirit and self-reflection!

You will preserve your *uniqueness and exceptionality* by using *the self -inductions* from this book that are meant to be instilled in your sub-conscious mind and imbue you with an unbreakable desire *to reveal the Best of You*!

The inspirational rhyming mind-sets and boosters will help this process to be internalized in you, *backing your spirit up, should it sag for any reason.*

Also, to become soul-wise, activate your love device!

To Life-Sustain, Give More Mental Food to the Brain!

2. We Are Here to Discover Ourselves!

You will not be overloaded with the redundant information here. All chunks of information in the book are ***page long,*** and they are information and technology friendly. I think that the avalanche of information that we are overwhelmed with these days needs to be thoroughly sifted in the brain for its validity for your personal or professional needs. After the information is selected, it gets connected to the chunks of information that are stored in your memory logically and consciously, enriching your intelligence and enlarging your outlook.

Generalize- Select - Internalize - Strategize – Actualize! Be Overly Wise!

I suggest you upload the mind-sets that best resonate with you into your smart phone in the file *Self-Resurrection*. Have them at hand as your **SELF-HELP THERAPY.** They will immediately uplift your mood, fortify your self-esteem, and boost your urge for action. The inspirational **Auto-Suggestive Methodology for Self-Ecology,** presented in this book is meant to help you do that. With the help of the auto -suggestibility - your personal auto-media, a sharpened self-perception of reality will be installed in you, and you will have a chance to enhance your immense creativity, expand your *"spiritualized intelligence"(Dr. Fred Bell)*, and develop high, DIGITALLY ENHANCED *self-consciousness that needs to have a visually installed structure in the brain.*

(Body+ Spirit+ Mind) + (Self-Consciousness + Universal Consciousness)

The religious paradigm that the humanity has been following for centuries has contributed a lot to our spiritual growth, but *we **have come to the point of no return in it*** because our religious differences are blinding us and pushing our personal growth to stagnation, stereotyped thinking, and dogmatic judgment. ***It is paramount now to reassess the reality in the light of the acquired religious wisdom together with new scientific development.*** In other words, we need to connect our piety-filled hearts with technologically advanced minds. Disconnection is the action of entropy, or the reflection of death! *So, a lot of intellectual and spiritual brewing must be done without sewing!*

In sum, the holistic personal evolution that I am talking about here is often side-tracked or neglected while it should be based on holistic awareness of the true realities of life and Self. It should be backed up with the SCIENCE OF LIFE.

Let's Reprogram our Brains without Vanity

from Religiousness to Spirituality!

3. Insert an Inspirational Virus into Your Being!

(An Inspirational Booster)

To consciously uplift your butt,

You need to inspirationally charge your gut!

> *Don't expect someone to inspire,*
>
> *To push you forward and emotionally rewire*

The messy mind's info

That had confused you before!

- - - - - - - - - - - - -

> *We blame the president, the loved ones, and a neighbor,*
>
> *Thus, directing the universal energy in our disfavor!*

The global informational war for the minds

Mushrooms in zillions of false files!

> *Everyone's blindly judging someone's mi-steps,*
>
> *While things done well are not at bets!*

But the lack of an inspirational virus is our fault,

And it needs to be willfully self-installed

> *From early childhood*
>
> *And with a good parenthood!*

Goodness can be properly sowed,

Only when we import

> *Some spiritual function*
>
> *For our inner construction!*

Then, the inspirational virus starts dispelling

The seeds of kindness and mercy dwelling!

Finally, by the time goodness gets installed,

A person matures into a spiritual patriot!

Dark consciousness that evil manifests

Stops being his or her pest!

A person becomes inwardly free

And, thus, obtains a higher self- consciousness glee!

Let's say to it, "So Be It!"

In our hearts and minds' beat!

Because to live long,

We must be very strong!

- - - - - - - - - - - - - - - - -

So, let's make the mind feel

And the heart perceives

The Power of "IS"

In its revealing bliss!

To illuminate our inner self-inflicted upsets,

We need new inspirational mind-sets!

Thus, the posture, a smile, and a good mood

Must always be our emotional food!

- - - - - - - - - - - - - - - -

Those that Defy the Gravity of the Common - Fly;

Those that Crawl - Die!

4. The Soul's Fitness is Our Spiritual Witness!

"Soul-Refining" is the book about spirituality of our souls that fortifies our mental-emotional fitness by focusing on soul-refining with the help of the *Inspirational Psychology for Self-Ecology.* Self- inspiration sharpens our aware attention to life and living and helps us realize our exceptionality.

"That which holds our attention, determines our action."(*W. James*)

Self-suggestibility is soul-repairing by way of injecting into the mind **auto-suggestive inspirational boosters and mind-sets** that resonate with any mind and soul because they reprogram the mind and sharpen aware attention to what is recognized by us as right. Since the psychologically charged messages in this book are very simple but persuasive, they better imbue a life-damaged soul with **"INTELLECTUALIZED SPIRITUALITY"** (*Dr. Fred Bell*) that promotes **heart + spirit + mind** awakening.

Let's intellectualize our hearts and emotionalize our minds!

The essential core of our souls - *body + spirit + mind* needs to be rewired into one inseparable unit, unique **I – CONCEPT** that is instilled in the brain by uploading the **authoritative inspirational support** that at the time of the exponential growth of information technology, we all need a lot.

Auto-Induction: *My aware attention is never in retention!*

In other words, soul refining is the work at conscious sculpturing and modifying oneself at the emotional level at the time of amazing digital transformation of life when our brains need more order and when our heads, more than ever, need to be in sync with our hearts. We must live by their indivisible unity that our inner barometer – **CONSCIENCE** tunes us up to, making our lives more conscientious and soul-refining. Soul-refining is also being more intelligent *to fight ignorance of the minds and the emptiness of the hearts* to make us more perceptive of the right turns in life.

The rightness of our behavior is being dictated by the rules of the society that are not the rules of life, or God, that is often interpreted by the society as the means of keeping the unruled people obeying the norms, inflicted on to them. Such situation is mostly connected with a sacred feeling of devotion and our *sincere love for the Superpower that we all call God and for each other,* irrespective of our sex, race, religious affiliation, or an administrative and financial status.

"Right is Might!" *(Richard Wetherill)*

5. Autosuggestibility Enhances this Ability!

If we want our souls to be fit, we need to learn to respect love in all its forms! Thousands of people suffer due to the heartless, prejudiced, limited attitude to love and living with love.

The search for a soulmate is a myth if you don't remove the love freeze!

We have numerous ancient ballads, tales, and novels in the classic wealth of the humanity about the breath-taking examples of love, destroyed by the broken norms of the society. "*Romeo and Juliet,* "*Anna Karenina,*" "*Madame Butterfly,*" etc. When and how do we expect to raise our children to have sacredness for true love if we keep killing it in our and their souls with the values degradation and the impersonal attitude to each other, hypocritically declaring, *God is love!*

The spirit of love is different at every time in history We will even have the artificial love, blossoming soon. A wonderfully made and played movie *"Her"* illustrates the future, and we respond inwardly to it because *our souls resonate to the inner music of the authenticity of such love.*

The ability to love determines the fitness of our souls!

Its vibrations are healthy, and such love, as love between many people, irrespective their religious affiliation, nationality, race, or sex preferences can be authentic *if it is sacred in the heart and the mind* and has nothing to do with the mass media reflection, the chase of money, or satisfying the whims of "immediate gratification." Such souls' love should never be destroyed by anyone's ignorant, love-dead, society-dictated perception of what is right or wrong. Every soul has its own cycle! *Any relationship ends; the questions are when and how.* The level of our **SELF-CONSCIOUSNESS** matters here more than any prejudices! Let love live, and let our souls be nourished with love!

Different, economic, political and social models are in fashion, and the time is adding new quality to our commonly shared life that is digitally monitored now. We are changing energy technologies and integrating them with our inner energy, transforming us and generating new INTELLIGENCE + SPIRITUALITY link. *"Without commitment, you'll never start; without consistency, you'll never finish!"* (Denzel Washington)
Change is in your range!

The Soul's Fitness is the Ability to Forestall Ignorance in Any Form!

6. Our Life's Equation is in the Spiritual Invasion!

Literally, life has a different quality depending on the state of our self-consciousness that changes *if we are in charge of the self-change creatively*. Transformation of self-consciousness into a constructive, not destructive force is our main goal on this path. So, I suggest you instill in your consciousness the **PLAN OF ACTION** for *Self-Installation* to inspire and modify the inner self.

<u>To conquer the world, go consciously and tirelessly forward!</u>

The book *"Soul-Refining"* presents the blueprint of such work <u>in the emotional dimension of self-development,</u> following the book *"I Am Free to Be the Best of M"* that features the self-transformational process <u>at the physical level</u>. *(See the holistic pyramid below)* The holistic structure that *five books on Self-Resurrection* present, from one level to the next, is meant to help you build life-awareness, self-sufficiency, and emotional stability in five dimensions of life, presented here.

The avalanche of information about what life is all about is too overwhelming now. So, I do my best <u>to present only the gist of it in page-long chunks of simplified and science -verified knowledge</u>.

We are all suggestible to some degree, and if we tend *to be self-suggesting* love, confidence, kindness, and compassion, we can uplift the spirit and do much more to ourselves than any most well-wishing therapist.<u></u>

<u>Soul-mending is taming the way we think, feel, speak, and act in five philosophical levels</u>: *mini, meta, mezzo, macro, and super,* or in the ***physical, emotional, mental, spiritual, and universal dimensions. T***o self-excel and become the best version of yourself, use **the AUTO-SUGGESTIVE METHODOLOGY OF SELF-ECOLOGY.**

We need to visualize the life's route to be always in a good mood:

The Holistic Paradigm of Self-Resurrection:

Physical Form + Spiritual Content of life

(Body+ Spirit+ Mind) + (Self-Consciousness + Universal Consciousness) =

A New, Whole, Spiritually Intellectualized Self!

<u>The Love of God is not just Granted; It is Earned!</u>

7. The Metrix of a Personality Formation is in our Emotional Transformation!

The books, mentioned in the scheme below comprise the **Holistic Paradigm of Self-Creation,** presenting the MANUAL OF LIFE, or the plan of action holistically. They are featuring five levels of self-growth <u>from bottom to top</u>. These stages, consequentially are: Self-Awareness, Self-Monitoring, Self-Installation, Self-Realization, and Self-Salvation.

The Holistic Self- Resurrection Pyramid:		Books, featuring these stages are:
5. Universal level	*Self-Salvation*	*"Beyond the Terrestrial!"*
4. Spiritual level	*Self-Realization*	*"Self-Taming!"*
3. Mental level	*Self-Installation -*	*"Living Intelligence of the Art of Becoming!"*
2. Emotional level	*Self-Monitoring*	*"Soul-Refining!"*
1. Physical level	*Self-Awareness*	*"I Am Free to Be the Best of Me!"*

There is no system without the structure!

The conceptual frame-work of these five books follows the structure of the Russian dolls, *Matryoshkas,* when one level incorporates the next one, forming one simple, ***holistic system of Self-Resurrection in life***, prompted by the present-day technological revolution and the necessity to adjust our personal pace with it *physically, emotionally, mentally, spiritually, and universally.*

Living Intelligence puts our intelligence in the working mode of the new reality <u>on the emotional level</u> that gets messed up by the overload of the information we get and the speed of life that we face. Consequently, it is instilling a new network of neurons in the brain, based on the technologically enhanced, ***holistically developing intelligence / self-consciousness.***

The book "***Soul-Refining***" presents the stage of Self-Monitoring that is essential for us in developing our "*emotional intelligence*" *(Daniel Goleman)*, or what I call EMOTIONAL DIPLOMACY, the lack of which stands in the way of our overall ***spiritual maturation***. *(See the book "Self-Taming"- spiritual level)*

A person on this path grows a new sense of identity, the identity of a person with "***spiritualized intelligence***", controlled emotions, a considerably raised self-consciousness, and the unity of the heart and the mind. ***A healthy emotional make up, or the spirit that is in the center of the holistic paradigm*** is an indispensable prerequisite for every soul on the path of Self - Resurrection.

"Self-Consciousness is the Product of Self-Creation!"*(Carl Yung)*

8. Multi-Dimensional Self-Creation is the Soul's Salvation!

The Path of the Holistic Self-Growth:

Super level	Super-Consciousness	*Self-Salvation*
Macro level	Self-Consciousness	*Self-Realization*
Mezzo level	Mind	*Self-Installation*
Meta level	Spirit	*Self-Monitoring*
Mini level	Body	*Self- Awareness*

Form   +   Content

(Body+ Spirit+ Mind) + (Self-Consciousness + Universal Consciousness)

= A New, Whole Self or our Intellectually Spiritualized

Human Fractal

(For more on the subject, see the book "I Am Free to Be the Best of Me!"- the initial, physical level of the Holistic Paradigm of Self-Creation.)

Embrace the Geology of Self-Ecology:

Levels:	Stages of Self-Creation:	Books:
5. *Universal level*	*Self-Salvation*	*"Beyond the Terrestrial!"*
4. *Spiritual level*	*Self-Realization*	*"Self-Taming!"*
3. *Mental level*	*Self-Installation*	*"Living Intelligence or the Art of Becoming"*
2. *Emotional level*	*Self-Monitoring*	*"Soul-Refining!'*
1. *Physical level*	*Self-Awareness*	*"I Am Free to Be the Best of Me!"*

www.language-fitness.com / See the video in the section Self-Resurrection

Our Life Fractals in Base are being Changed in Time and Space!

24

9. The Self-Suggestive Philosophy of Soul-Refining

Next, let me make one point, connected with the title of this book, crystal clear. It's not a book of a religious mind-set, or spooky interactions with dead souls. It is the book about the INDUCTIVE PSYCHO CULTURE of *self-ecology,* based on the important aspects of the mind– *inspiration, praying, and intuition.*

Self-suggestibility is, in fact, a self-fulfilling prophesy.

The book is about *self-trained life-awareness*, self-boosted will-power, renewed self-sufficiency, strengthened self-confidence, and refreshed self-love.

Self-Induction: ***In my mind, I am One of a kind!***

The holistic philosophy that I back up my ideas with is meant to strengthen your ***mental-emotional fitness*** and help you get in touch with your soul through constant soul-refining that we all need to do daily at every conscious moment.

Our life goal is to make ourselves whole!

I suggest focusing on soul-refining with the help of the INSPIRATIONAL PSYCHOLOGY for SELF-ECOLOGY (*Self- Hypnosis*) that I have tried to *introduce and explore in my previously published books.* The main concepts of this book are illustrated with rhyming inspirational, psychologically- backed up boosters and mind-sets that are easily memorized and technologically friendly.

Self-suggestibility in the form of timely self-therapy is recommended to be applied by instilling in the mind ***the rhyming auto-inductions, or programs*** that discipline thinking and act as psychological injections for alert awareness and aware attention to be called to action at the time of our fast-digital emersion that is causing an evolutionary transformation of our brains at the cellular level. *(Dr. Bruce Lipton).*

The biological software still prevails in our brains, and we need to enhance it with the help of the technological means before the artificial intelligence will take the lead.

Download the mind-sets you need into the smart phone to mind-feed.

The mistakes that we make in life make up the experience that we get. It is gradually transforming into ***wisdom as a conscious, holistic, reasonable vision of life.*** Build it up in yourself with auto-inductions that fortify the character and put the heart and mind in sync. As *King Solomon's* wisdom states,

"As People Think in Their Hearts, so They Are!"

10. Your Life's Force is in Being Your Own Boss!

As I have mentioned above, self-inducting is done with the help of ***the rhyming word with a psychological filling*** that is creating its own supporting reality. If the needed boosters are stored in the brain, they pop up in the mind at the right time and at any place. The authoritative command to the mind, given in the form of a rhyming inspirational booster, <u>changes the train of thought in the right direction</u> and makes a person more life-fit in a challenging situation.

To be less life-beat, become more life-fit!

Other than that, the rhyming inspirational auto-inductions, retrieved from the memory and injected into the mind at the right moment, act also as the timely psychological remedy, or ***a self-help mind-application.*** All you need to do is to store a couple of self-help inspirational boosters in your smart phone, file Self-Resurrection, ***like first-aid prayers,*** and inwardly command yourself to follow the rhyming instruction, if need be. For instance, just saying the auto-induction below, you will note the difference in your spirit and self-confidence that we all <u>need to choreograph every conscious moment</u>.

I am my best friend; I am my "Beginning and my End"!

This command immediately changes your mind-set, reminding you of your own personal value and self-sufficiency, and it imbues you with the ability to deal with any problem because you are strong and smart enough for it! This command immediately resonates with your emotional make-up and boosts your spirit to decision-making that your another friend – INTUITION prompts to you at that moment. You may even fortify your spirit with one more booster to back up the one, mentioned above.

In my life quest, I manifest the best!

Inspirational boosting always uplifts the mood, strengthens the willpower, and wakes us up to the **"AS IS"** reality, as opposed to the wishful reality that impulsivity engraves in us, generating irritability, anger, and a lot of frustration.

Self-Induction: <u>Right is My Might</u> *(Richard Wetherill, "Right is Might!).*

In sum, our hunger for knowledge and the urge for self-boosting based on science-verified knowledge, as well as the desire <u>to be personable and able to accomplish</u> <u>full self-realization in life,</u> is a life-long need, and I want to share mine with those who aspire to do so. As *Leo Vygotsky* wrote,

"The Personality is a Unique Role Play of the Soul!"

11. Everything Happens for a Reason

To prove my point, let me tell you how it all started. Most unexpectedly, I began writing rhyming inspirational boosters and mind-sets to help my daughter after **September 11, 2001** attack in which, Yolanta, a very successful, 21-year old college graduate, had miraculously survived while her five friends died.

Having been in the very turmoil of human life destruction, she lost any desire to live and was totally in the grips of fear and frustration. Both of us had no medical insurance at that time, and I felt a desperate need to use my knowledge of the brain as a psycholinguist to ease her trauma and help her forget the horrors of that day. The situation demanded my doing something out of the ordinary. Yolanta needed *alert awareness to be installed in her brain* to bring back the desire to live without fear, awful visual imprints, and most depleting desperation that needed the influx of much emotional gas.

Then, one day, while driving, I felt that my *thoughts were rhyming into the psychologically charged messages* that kept coming to my mind, demanding that I stop the car and write them down because the memory erased them then and there. Like *Neale Donald Walsh*, who had started his amazing conversations with God out of the blue, I began writing the rhyming inspirational boosters as if dictated to me from the Above, marveling at myself and mostly at the fact that *the stanzas of the boosters got cut in a rap-like way.* It was even more baffling to me because I hated rap at that time. I am a scholar, an academically minded and very disciplined woman who had never written a lyrical line in her life. And there I was, rhyming, philosophizing, and rationalizing about life.

When I came home, I wrote down the first auto-suggestive product of my mind on a small kitchen board. Yolanta was more than impressed and unexpectedly responsive to it. Obviously, the brightest intellect and the most stable psyche *(she had always been a very bright and shiny girl before)* are not immune to human vulnerability. Thus, I taught her to boost her spirit auto-suggestively, inspiring her *to keep resisting, rejecting, and reforming* herself from inside.

Since then, I never stopped writing inspirational psychologically backed up boosters to uplift myself, my students, and anyone who visits my webpage, seeking life support to boost his / her spirit and enthuse oneself and others.

Thus, from the Beginning,
I started Writing Hymns to Living and Being!

12. Self-Hypnosis is the Best Life Prognosis!

Someday, Somehow,

Everything Will Be Better

than Now!

Somehow, Someday,

Everything will be

Okay!

The rhyming inspirational, boosters and mind-sets (the authoritative mind-programming self-inductions here) *are meant to <u>illustrate the book's main concepts in a poetic, psychologically grounded form</u> They will uplift your spirit and help you rationalize your life with it. Choose the mind-sets that resonate with you most and upload them into your smart phone to have them at hand as a psychological support.*

Technologically incentivize your brain. Be mindful and sane!

<u>"If you practice gratitude, you'll become grateful!"</u>

(Joe Dispenza)

Be Self-Governable, Not Mass Media Programmable!

(I Practice what I Preach with my Inspirational Outreach!)

The Soul's Trinity is in the Universal Life's Infinity!

Trinity is the Divine Potentiality of our Human Exceptionality!

Use digital technology for Self-Ecology!

Upload your smart phone with a new inspirational tone.

Inspiration, Praying, and Intuition are Your Soul's Fruition!

1. The Soul's Trinity

In the universal infinity,

<u>The soul has its own trinity!</u>

It constitutes a link

<u>Of the body, the spirit, and the mind in sync!</u>

The spirit, the mind, and the body

Are the trinity that embodies

Our deepest dreams

And many uncontrolled whims!

A soul's trinity

Is always in unity!

The soul talks to the mind;

The mind monitors the brain;

The brain operates the body in a tight rein

And energizes every cell's vein!

We've lived in this trinity

For an infinity!

And when we die,

<u>The trinity governs us to the hell or Rai!</u> (Russian for heaven)

The downward process goes in reverse

To let the soul be reborn on the planet Earth!

When the body dies,

The brain follows its mortal advice

<u>The mind picks the info</u>

<u>And pushes the soul up therefore!</u>

The velocity of this metamorphosis

Keeps eternity in process!

> *So, to stay in a good soul's health,*
>
> *You need to enlarge your mind's wealth!*

Your role is to energize the heart and the mind,

To push the soul up for a new rewind!

> *Thus, the Trinity of the soul*
>
> *Helps us commit to our evolutionary goal!*

- - - - - - - - - -

Holistic Paradigm of the Soul's Salvation

Form   +   Content

(Body+ Spirit+ Mind) + (Self-Consciousness + Universal Consciousness)

= The Whole, Intellectually Spiritualized Soul!

Speaking in spiritual terms, **the Trinity** for me is the unity of the Divine Mother (or the **Body**, *giving life to us - the Earth*) - the **Spirit - Jesus Christ**, or *any spiritual leader that you might follow*, and the **Mind - God,** or *the Universal Intelligence that is governing us in every cell.*).

The Trinity is an unbreakable unity of life's infinity!

The form of life, represented by the unbreakable unity of the body, spirit, and the mind, imbued with **the spiritual volume** of life (*self-consciousness connected to the Universal Consciousness*) <u>**constitute the wholeness of the soul**</u> that we need to construct in us, sculpturing our unique souls so that we could prove our exceptionality in giving the world the best we have.

The Trinity's Conceptual Paradigm is in

the Heart + Spirit + Mind's Twine!

2. We No Longer Have the Luxury of Ignorance!

The Old Knowledge Becomes

Obscene

on the Technological Life's

Scene!

"Our Consciousness is evolving; our DNA is getting re-programmed, and the Enlightenment is increasing."

(Davis Wilcock)

With more awareness about life, we need to stop faking it, stop playing games with other people, stop rehearsing life as if thinking that one day, we'll live it for real.

Realization of the sacredness of life in our minds and hearts is the conceptual meaning of our new digitally enhanced REVELATION that is the core message of any sacred book and that is perceived deeper and more insightfully by the humanity from generation to generation.

Our technological age demands each of us become

a Soul-Refined Spiritual Sage!

.

Don't Let Your Soul Repose and Decompose!

3. All that Glitters is Not Gold!

We are often told,

"All that glitters is not gold!"

           A guy that makes a ton of money

           Seems to be shiny but is a dummy!

A girl that's beautiful and funny

Is far from being a great mummy.

           A child that's cute and nice

           Grows up to be an entire farce!

A boss that seems to be professionally equipped

Turns out to be a very bad fit!

           Or a seemingly harmonious marital bliss

           Can often reveal much nasty soul's grease.

We like to judge a book by its cover,

Without probing into its inner Mer-Ka-Ba.

           But the book that's worth reading

           Has the capacity for weaving

The threads of kindness and wisdom

That glitter within a soul's charisma

           Because only a constantly refined mold

           Can transform coarse metal into shiny gold!

You Radiate what You Emanate!

4. Before You See with Your Eyes

An Inspirational Booster)

Before you see with your eyes

And hear with your ears,

> *Perceive with your soul*

> *And change your life's goal*

From a negative life eruption

To the spiritual dimension!

> *Thank God for the bitter and for the sweet,*

> *For both make your life complete!*

Only with God in your heart and the mind

Are you ready to unwind

> *All the problems in front of you*

> *And behind!*

To Be One with God's Mind,

Be One of a Kind!

5. Live in Balance with All!

(An Inspirational Booster)

Adversity reveals,

Prosperity conceals

   Our best talents and funs

   That the God grants!

We complain

That we can't sustain

   The pressure of His demands

   And absence of any refunds!

But when we were born,

God defines the form

   Of our contribution

   To the final life's solution!

Were you wise,

What have you realized?

   If you get prosperity free,

   You'll pay for it triple in fee!

But if you earned it with zest,

In a tough life's quest,

   If you give out the gifts

   That God reveals

Back in the bits

Of your best talent's fits,

God grants you with the soul's wealth

As a deserved result of your life's quest!

So, live in balance with all

That God had originally installed!

And be worthy of His Word

To get a High Approval reward!

The Soul's Conceptual Paradigm is
in the Heart, the Spirit, and the Mind's Twine!

"If your heart is wise, my heart will rejoice!!"

(Proverb 23. 15)

Instill the visual picture of the whole of you to clean the soul's milieu.

The Form + The Content of Life = We go beyond survive!

(Body+ Spirit+ Mind) + (Self-Consciousness+ Universal Consciousness)

= A New, Holistically- developing Self!

Auto-induction:

Don't Be Mindlessly Automatic;

Be Soul-Aristocratic!

6. Preserve Your Soul's Symphony!

(An Inspirational Booster)

Be illuminated and calm

And don't let any human scum

> *Disturb your inner symphony*
>
> *With his or her mental cacophony.*

Being unique and not soul-bleak

Is the hardest job to seek!

> *It requires a lot of charisma,*
>
> *That's immune to anyone's "criticisma"*

Many will rain

On your soul's terrain!

> *But if you are wall strong.*
>
> *You'll be able to forestall*

Any emotional intrusion

With your heart + spirit + mind fusion!

> *Thus, you'll get illuminated and calm*
>
> *And enjoy the music of the life's fun!*

"Life is the rhythm that you need to tune up to."

(Nikola Tesla)

Change the Attitude to Raise your Soul's Altitude!

7. Live Consciously!

(An Inspirational Booster)

There is only one out-

   come

For everyone under the

   Sun!

If you want to be above the

   Ground,

Keep yourself happy and

   Sound!

Your cells are the people of your bodily estate.

Keep them active and healthily innate!

Also, defy the gravity of your

   Age

With a firm and graceful

   Rage,

And accept your life in its entire

   Mass,

For it, too, shall

   Pass!

"Live Consciously! Consciousness Mobilizes!"

(Neale Donald Walsch)

8. The Art of Living is in the Art of Soul-Thriving, Not Just Surviving!

To Be More Life-Fit,

Constantly

Self-Uplift!

Your Life Stops Running when You

Start Whining!

Don't Ever Compromise Yourself

with the Self-Betraying

Evil Spell!

Your time is limited, and the sand-clock of your life should go in portions of kindness, love, and mindedness, not in a mass of the emotional mess, all at once in a fun recess!

Lifetime – Do Not Whine!

9. Soul Refining Needs Self-Redefining!

Intelligence + Awareness = Living Intelligence!

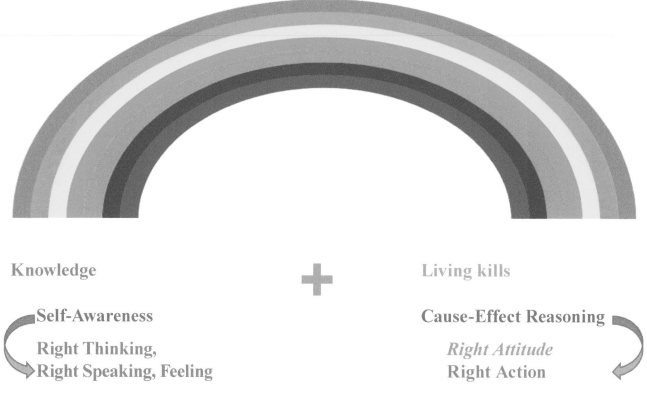

Knowledge   +   Living kills

Self-Awareness   Cause-Effect Reasoning

Right Thinking,   *Right Attitude*
Right Speaking, Feeling   Right Action

== Higher Consciousness and Perpetual Happiness

Every piece of knowledge, holistically presented in this book, is sifted for its validity and is correlated in the over-arching way to be easily digestible and technologically friendly. Living at the age that is modifying and simulating human intelligence demands that we become *a conscious part of this exponentially growing process* of our integration into a new, very complicated reality. To fit into it, we must be soul fit!

(Body+ Spirit+ Mind) + (Self-Consciousness + Universal Consciousness)
= The Whole Intellectually Spiritualized Soul!

You can find zillions of motivational talks on the Internet, given by many successful people, celebrities, scientists, and gurus, but you'll be able to make them real only if you **GENERALIZE, SELECT,** and **ACTUALIZE** them yourself, following the holistic paradigm of Self-Installation. **This is what this book is all about!**

Our Common Goal is the Renaissance of the Soul!

Halleluiah to Our Spiritual Stem
from the Times of Eden!

Beauty's Elation is Always Life's Declaration!

Grains of Me
and My
Philosophy!

Strengthen the Potentiality of your Exceptionality!

(From duality to the holistic unity!)

Personal Evolution is the Solution!

1. Information ⟶ Transformation!

For millennia, civilization depended on the information we got from *the Above*, and the consequences of its right / wrong interpretation either maximized or minimized the speed of our spiritual and intellectual evolution. *New education presupposes new self-awareness and new training for life!* I think that we need to stop arguing about religion and start viewing life, uniting every conceptual difference of our definitions of God, the manifestation of *the One Universal Living Being*, under one common thought that science is generating in our minds as:

the Universal Intelligence, the Creator, the Absolute, the Consciousness of the Universe, or the Master Mind.

Through the process of understanding, we will be in permanent transformation into beings who are *wiser and more conscious.* Dead knowledge or inflated intelligence forms only biological robots, not critical thinking beings that evolution depends on. Our present-day youth has no centers of self-development, nor is it the goal of our educational institutions.

Their personality growth is being done in a blind pursuit of an illusionary goal that rarely gets totally realized often due to the social and financial restrictions. Their personal interaction choices are limited to the Internet virtual friendships, bars, drugs and alcohol, or any other social groups that are mostly fun-oriented. True leaders are self-sufficient and not dependent on social groups. They seek the like-minded, creative, advanced people that are pursuing the goal of giving the world the best they have.

There are many goal-oriented, beautiful young people who seek their goals and find. However, there are many more lost young minds who need guidance to be self-creation oriented on the path of getting a lot of self-education and achieving *professional Self-Installation.* They want to be inspired by the best minds and creative personalities like those of *Steve Jobs, Bill Gates, and Elon Musk* to revolutionize the picture of our evolutionary Now.

A self-creation process that each of us is going through willingly or randomly during the life time is, in fact, our getting more aware of the ever changing conceptual structure of the reality in which each soul counts because it is a part of the whole - *the Consciousness of God, the Universal Light* that we are learning to tap into, getting charged by it and reflecting it digitally..

"Human Perception is Merely Light Perceiving Light"

(Don Miguel Ruiz)

2. Time is Gliding Fast Away - No Dismay!

Following the demands of artificial intelligence that is governing our evolutionary development and that has already started modifying our minds and hearts in an exponential way, *our individual and social roles are changing radically now.* But <u>we cannot afford to lose our human exceptionality,</u> our incredible ability to love, feel compassion display care and kindness, embracing our fellow humans with the nobleness of our intentions to feel for the other, *not just think for the other.*

The automatism of our actions and absence of rationality in them are appalling now, and it is the duty of each of us to preserve our souls' and enrich them with the qualities that a machine will not be capable of reproducing for quite some time.

"The one who does not save himself, condemns himself."

The intention to obtain a perfect **HEART + MIND EQUILLIBRIUM** is innate in us, and we need to restore it. The wellness of our robotized souls should be in harmony with the inner music that is vibrating in us.

"I am light and music in a human form!"(Nikola Tesla)

The unforgettable words of Mather Luther King *"I have a dream,"* remind us of his belief in the human potential. I hope that one day we will *have free centers for self-development* all over the world. I hope that they will serve as the *universal launching platforms,* or the steppingstones for the young generation into the *physical, emotional, mental, spiritual, and universal self- resurrection* within their lifetime. *(See the book "Beyond the Terrestrial!")*

One thing should be stable and unarguable in our search of this dream. We need to GALVANIZE *the spirit* and RAISE *our consciousness* every minute, hour, day, month, year in five dimensions, presented in the main parts of the book, <u>five Soul-Refining Stages</u> consistently and irrespective of the unfavorable circumstances that are the *regular fluctuations of light - darkness* and *success – failure* cast at us..

The ongoing process of information-transformation is a never-ending philosophical paradigm at work: *Synthesis – Analysis - Synthesis!*

Necessity ⟶ *Intention* ⟶ *Actualization!*

Self-Synthesis – Self-Analysis – Self-Synthesis!

3. The Mind Talks, the Brain Works!

There are no shortcuts in achieving such *five- dimensional self- transformation and soil-refining.* We must be willing to work hard for it by stretching our minds, refining our souls, and becoming much better human beings <u>physically, emotionally, mentally, spiritually, and universally.</u> *Departmentalize your knowledge* of yourself and of life in these dimensions!

Be self-disciplined, dynamic, and consciously- conscious!

Dead souls do not have a profound sense of mission; they just follow the common narrative of life. Only with our extended intelligence in sync with interior and exterior goodness, enriched by artificial intelligence, can we push the human evolution to the top stage of consciousness:

Super-Consciousness and *Super-Intelligence are yet in negligence!*

The chase for money, material adornment, and an automatic lifestyle have generated indifference, political correctness, and petty- mindedness. Many people, focused on one thing - money, are deaf and blind to the voice of reason, compassion, and true intelligence. *But there is no perfection in matter since matter is subject to transformation.* This transformation demands much life awareness and the clarity of thinking that in turn necessitates the clarity of the soul that is demonstrating tact, manners, patience., contentment, and life-respect.

<u>Soul-refinement is to be secured from the within!</u>

The inner work is a separate skill to be developed through active – *Auto-Suggestive* and passive *- Transcendental or Yoga Meditations* that help us establish the link between the mind and the heart and put them in synch with the Universal Intelligence. We need operative, conscious, and heart-based processing of the in-coming information to transmit it adequately to other human beings through our telepathically connected souls. Only such interaction constitutes our growing consciousness, based on mental-emotional intelligence, positivity, kindness, and purity of the souls. I remember another piece of wisdom that my mom kept reminding me of when I was too much in a hurry, *"Be in a hurry only for one reason - to do good to someone without treason."*

Each Soul, as such, is One with the Universal Intelligence at Large!

4. If It's to Be, It's Up to Thee!

The new, technologically enhanced times demands that we develop" *spiritualized intelligence" (Dr. Fred Bell)* – the newly informed spirituality and a new understanding of ourselves as unique human beings with a singular mission in life. There are many exceptionally-advanced thinkers in the world – philosophers, scientists, gurus that have established the communication with *the Universal Intelligence*, that we call God, each in his own, singular way.

In such cases, the process of *personal synthesis* takes place at a new level of enlightenment, self-worth, and self-realization. The man who has stepped on the path of *re-inventing himself by acquiring new life-awareness*, stops being a part of the *"collective unconscious."* The process of Self-Installation for such person is always consciously - governed by the holistic paradigm:

Self- Synthesis - Self-Analysis - Self-Synthesis!

Personal integrity of such people is incredible, and their souls operate at much higher vibrations. They are *the beacons of self-growth* for all of us. An amazing book *"Flower of Life"* by a great, non-traditional thinker *Drunvalo Melchizedek* who is a mine of wisdom and integrity presents the concept of a human exceptionality, demonstrating *the role of the sacred geometry* in the life structure and the universal framework, **THE MER-KA-BAH.**

In God's mind, we are One with the universal kind!

Note please, the lack of individualized and personalized frame of thought is detrimental for self-refining. The lack of a solid self-image only leads to an ignorant automatic living, devoid of real spirituality and self-growth. The *Science of Mer-ka-bah* is revealing to us that we accelerate the pace of our conscious life learning to finally obtain strong *personal magnetism* that makes other people gravitate to our knowledge, charisma, and motivation.

"Man, as a being of sense, wants his life to make more sense."(Alan Watts)

It becomes an achievable goal if "*the right amount of effort is used in the right direction and if we use technology to enrich our cognition.*". *(Ray Kurzweil)* In other words, we need to think, feel, and live spiritually, without anyone's malicious intent to redirect our effort or stop it economically or politically. A famous statement" *If it's to be, it's up to me!*" is at work here, because

There Wasn't, There Isn't, and There Won't Ever Be Anyone Like Me!

Don't Let Your Soul Get Dry and Hole!

Ниагарский водопад без воды, 1969 год.

Think how to Soul-Refine,

Don't Be like the Niagara Falls in1969!

5. Don't Be Soul -Negligent; Be Soul-Intelligent!

Without the strategic plan of action that we need to keep in mind, our *souls are getting dry and blind!* A great American Project of 1996 *to dewater* American Falls was finally stopped and declared to be sufficiently unstable because it was agreed that the waterfall should not be stabilized by artificial means.

By analogy, *our brains and hearts are being dried out and sanitized by both mass media and the artificial intelligence*, and we must forestall both knowingly! The world is getting better by every measure in many spheres of life, but our natural empathy, compassion, kindness, and love are becoming more and more dried out. *Our souls should not be de-spiritualized by the technological invasion into our minds and hearts!* Artificial intelligence is a great wonder of our time that is meant to enrich us intellectually, emotionally, and spiritually, and on these premises, *we should evolve into much more noble beings.*

The process of soul-refining means that we take care of <u>the impersonal attitude that corrodes the soul and dries out our hearts of love, compassion, and care.</u> The attitude of indifference hits the soul right into the heart and breaks the most vital connection between the heart and the mind of a person. Our automatic reaction, *"I don't care; What do I care ; Whatever; Leave me alone,"* etc. dry up the soul of its spiritual fluids and emotional energy. These energies can hardly become replaceable unless we consciously enact the forces of the emotional revival and soul-refining. Each of us needs *to tune his / her inner musical instrument, the soul*, to the vibrations of the Earth as a living organism.

> *"Spirituality is measured by the sound of good thoughts and kind actions, ot by a religious label."* (Leo Tolstoy)

Only the most perceiving and mind-bold ones can *creatively respond to the free energy of the spirit* that the entire Universe is so generously radiating and that the most soul-refined and advanced thinkers can tap, pushing our civilization to the unbelievable heights of the impossible. Let's appreciate their contribution!

<u>Let's honor every heart and the mind that are not universally blind!</u>

What to know and how to apply this knowledge to bettering the world is the path of any soul on Earth! In his wonderful novel," *For Whom the Bell Tolls,"* Ernest Hemingway wrote, *"It tolls for you!"* Our responsibility for the inner integrity is being tolled from inside. and outside.

"Earth Rings as a Bell!" (Nikola Tesla)

6. Stagnation Cannot Be the Source of the Soul's Elation!

Undoubtedly, the hardest work to do is the work at oneself, and **an auto-suggestive back-up** will be very helpful for you on the path of your emotional evolution. **Self-growth needs to be self-monitored with self-support and a positive self-regard**. One needs to become his own best-trusted ally, talking to his peculiar *"I am"* directly and supporting it, if need be, with the *inspirational injections* and *authoritative commands* that boost the spirit and fill it up with rationality, enthusiasm, love of life, and determination for action.

I am my best friend; I am my "Beginning and my End"!

Of course, if you happen to already be a perfect person, quite content with who you are, this book is not for you. **Soul-recovery** is for those who feel the demand of the present-day times **to dematerialize their souls**, who witness their deteriorating values, experience indifference to what is going on in the world and feel an impersonal attitude to each other. That's why **LOVE** is often mistaken for **FAST PASSING ATTRACTION** of a one-night stand.

Our life roles are eroded by a massive disconnection of the souls!

We put the blame for our depleted, life-damaged souls on an exponential growth of the technological giant that is looming now over our personal and professional lives. We blame our emotional and mental turmoil on the rush of life, the politicians, the adversarial religion, the national characteristics of a person, or his / her skin color, etc. Meanwhile, there are thousands of people who prove that their self-growth is not obstructed by those factors, and *their magnetic spiritually intelligent fields* glue them to the path of self-resurrection, fortified by the avalanche of information that they technologically-digest. It is possible for them because they truly monitor their minds and lives themselves.

Many of us are not life-fit because we are soul-beat!

But whatever the posture the life puts you in, **don't stoop**. Stand up beautiful and tall! The right time to be better and stronger never comes because every time we have an urge **to discover the paradise within** is the right time! *The giants of spirit are the giants of consciousness!* They generate in us the desire *to create beauty and order in ourselves and in the world*. I quote many of them, and they all share their wisdom on the Internet. (*See the book "Love Ecology," 2020*)

The Growth of Self-Worth is Not for Human Moths!

7. Don't Let Your Soul Repose and Decompose!

Don't let your soul repose,
Or get decomposed!
Keep it from decay,
Night and Day!

The inner dignity of the whole
Forms the aristocratism of your soul!

So, defy the gravity
Of a common-sense thought
And fly to the stars,
No matter what!

Integrate Yourself in Every Cell! Put the Pieces of the Puzzle of Your Life Together!

Souls Do Not Die; They Relive and Thrive!

Life is a Structured Entity of the Infinity!

8. The Cultivation of the Mind and Character

In sum, below, in the up-coming five main parts of the book, **five Stages** featuring five dimensions: ***physical, emotional, mental, spiritual, and universal, I explore soul-refining*** accordingly in the <u>*Mini. Meta, Mezzo, Macro, and Super* levels</u> of self-creation holistically. These are the levels that I present in my five books on Self- Resurrection, **focusing on soul-refining** stem at each stage of the holistic self-growth

<u>Soul-Refining is Self-Redefining!</u>

Self-Knowledge (ve), Self-Monitoring (Part Six), Self-Installation, (Part Seven), Self-Realization (Part Eight), and Self-Salvation (Part Nine).

<u>The Holistic Paradigm of Soul -Resurrection:</u>

Super level	**Super-Consciousness**	*Self-Salvation*
Macro level	**Self-Consciousness**	*Self-Realization*
Mezzo level	**Mind**	*Self-Installation*
Meta level	**Spirit**	*Self-Monitoring*
Mini level	**Body**	*Self- Awareness*

<u>*Body+ Spirit+ Mind + Self-Consciousness+ Universal Consciousness*</u>

= A New, Holistically Developed Self!

We are now at the early stage of our ***Living Intelligence, bringing together our biological and digital systems.*** As a matter of fact, soul-refining and the development of ***the Living Intelligence Skills*** have been my life occupation for thirty years of my academic work, and I am proud to have instilled these skills in thousands of my students from all over the world. The result of my work on their ***soul-refining and self-installation*** has been verified by my many students' totally transformed and self-realized lives that complete my own self-realization. I think that self-suggestibility plays a vital soul-repairing and self-inspiring role

Everyone on Earth needs the support of self-worth!

It is, in fact, a life-saving skill that ***unearths a person's psychological needs*** to be timely addressed by the person himself. Our self-talk never ends, and the choice of words that we use to empower ourselves determines the mental and emotional framework of our lives. The folk wisdom states:

"Be Careful what you wish for You Might Get it!"

9. For the Reader to Consider

To Raise Self-Consciousness means to Change the Mind!

The mental dimension of soul-refinement, **Stage Three** below, features ten steps of holistic Intelligence development

5. Universal Dimension	*Universal Intelligence*	
	Spiritual Intelligence	
4. Spiritual Dimension	*Social Intelligence*	
	Cultural Intelligence	
3. Mental Dimension)	*Financial Intelligence*	
	Professional Intelligence	
2. Emotional Dimension -	*Psychological Intelligence*	
	Emotional Intelligence.	
1. Physical Dimension	*Language Intelligence*	
	General Intelligence	

*See the Global Excellence award winning book / March 2020 -"**Living Intelligence or the art of becoming!** / www.language-fitness.com*

Intellectual self-perfection is a lifetime job that **is SELF-CONSCIOUSNESS IN ACTION**, the consciousness that is constantly ***self-educated, willfully cultivated, and updated!*** Spiritual maturation goes on in a fractal form.

Spiritual Fractals of Self-Symmetry:

Universal Level	Oneness (*Inner unity with all life*)
Spiritual level	Grace (*Conscious faith, nobleness*)
Mental level	Mind (*Spiritualized intelligence*)
Emotional level	Spirit (*Blissfulness, will-power*)
Physical level	Body (*Self-awareness, energy, wellness*)

(Body+ Spirit+ Mind) + (Self-Consciousness + Universal Consciousness)

(The physical form) + *(the spiritual content of life)*

"Don't Be Vexed, Be Humbled. Victory is on the Way!"

(Winston Churchill)

10. Be Soul-Blessed and Life-Obsessed!

Self-Induction:

Soul Salvation is in My Inner Spiritual Maturation!

<u>Accumulate the spiritual might</u> *in the second, third, fourth, fifth, sixth, seventh, eighties, ninth, and one hundredth* <u>cycles of your life.</u>

Be a self-reforming optimist! Don't let the devils inside defeat your soul's might!

Alongside with the rhyming inspirational boosters and mind-sets that are supposed to charge you with more love of life, I present below the grains of my auto-suggestive philosophy in page-long chunks of information on soul-refining, spirituality, and self-forming actuality <u>to boost your digitally enhanced intelligence.</u> Science proves that the Universal Intelligence is monitoring our minds. **Dr. Steven Weinberg**, *the Nobel prize winner*, ascertains our common goal on the path of self-evolution in life, saying,

"We Need to Trust the Universal Intelligence and Live in Unity with It!"

11. "No Soul is Left Behind!"

(Edgar Cayce)

For the developing mind,
"No soul is left behind!"

The spark of goodness lies within every soul,
And finding the purpose of life instills this goal!

The principle of One and Oneness directs our lives;
We are God's co-creators, kind and wise!

Like life's material manifestation,
We become more God-centered in soul re-formation!

Thus, the purpose for each other
Is "to be the light onto another!"

"If we cannot eliminate the bad in us,
We should illuminate the best!"

(Leo Vygotsky)

For Your Soul's Elation, Stop the Evil Autointoxication!

May then the Omnipresent God

Take you off the sign "STOP!"

And release you into the Life Stream,

as perfect as His every Creation Seam!

(Body+ Spirit+ Mind) + (Self-Consciousness + Universal Consciousness)

= A new Intellectually Spiritualized You!

Life Reverence is in the Living Intelligence!

Let's Soul-Philosophize to Become Wise!

Our Universal Goal is to Humanize the Soul!

"Wisdom belongs to those who seek advice."

(Proverbs 13,10)

Use Technology for Your Self-Ecology!

(Upload your smart phone with a new Soul-Refining tone!)

Magnify Nobility and Positivity in Your Mind; Be One of a Kind!

1. A New Conceptual Content of Life

Life in its indescribable beauty and variety desperately needs to be respected and carefully preserved in each of us, irrespective of the economic and political hullabaloo that affects us all, *making us unable to resist, reject, and reform its evil form!* We should not be the victims of the reality.

We must manage it and re-form it in sync with *the Universal Stream of Consciousness* that we need to learn to tap digitally now, as immortal careers of this consciousness.

THE SCIENCE OF LIFE that I advocate for is supposed <u>to provide a simple plan of action, the blueprint of self-development</u> in the *physical, emotional, mental, spiritual, and universal realms of life* **at least at the dilettante level,** forming the holistic and much more adequate picture of the reality in our minds, making us **SELF-AWARE** science-wise.

The situation prompted by our incredible leap in technological development requires "**A NEW CULTURE OF THINKING**" (Dr. *Fred Bell)* that demands our rationalization of life, reviewing of our materialistic values, and getting rid of bad, life-conditioned habits of judging, and begrudging.

<u>Humanization of the soul is everyone's personal goal!</u>

Everything is acceptable and explainable now, and the souls of our young people are twisted with shamelessness, gameness, love-lessness, and rudeness. We substitute the eternal soul's values of maternity and father's love, care, support, and the eternal sense of family responsibilities with the talks about tolerance and <u>acceptances of anything that mass media presents as a norm of life</u>. Love has a kaleidoscope of differences and shades, but its true essence remains the same, and it needs to be respected by us, without trying to please the new social breeze and the wish to go with the flow.

I'm not a prude, and I respect true feelings in the same sex marriages *as a free expression of the heart + mind connection*, but not its evil social reflection, demonstrated at the ugly gay parades, and other clone-like distortions of the beauty of the soul. that only mar the authenticity of feelings that some people have the right to have. *Albert Einstein* qualified precisely such *lack of soul connection between people* and their indulgence into what traditional religion used to qualify as sin, saying

"Bad Habits have a Good Tendency - either you Kill Them, or they Kill You."

2. The Science of Life and the Living Skills

In view of the information outlined above, a new subject that could raise our intelligence - consciousness and develops our **LIVING SKILLS** is needed to be studied by us from birth and during the entire life. ***This subject may be***

"The Science of Life", or "The Mastery of Life."

The universe is alive. Its sacred power, the Universal Mind, is the matrix of all being. The Science of Life is supposed to present life at large in its indescribable beauty and variety, but with the ***simplicity that is much more difficult to be accomplished*** than complexity that we bump into in every area of our red tape topped life. We, as well as our kids, need to be aware of the twists and turns in the search of new life-awareness to figure out who we are in the vast Universal infinity

But the Science of Life should not be overloaded with scientific details.

It needs to be constantly renewed, presenting the latest breakthroughs in science ***in the most digestible way,*** inciting the young minds with revolutionizing ideas, presented simply, but intriguingly so they could stimulate their indigo minds. As the Nobel Prize Winner *Dr. Steven Weinberg* puts it, ***"The increasing simplicity in the description of nature points to the fact that the final theory of everything is very simple and beautiful."***

The Science of Life should also be ***holistic in its structure*** with a much more simplistic and logically presented descriptions of the Laws of the Nature than we have at present. My heart is bleeding at seeing our kids stoop under the weight of the manuals that they carry on their backs, never actually being able to even look through half of those mines of knowledge.

"Almost every push-button device should introduce new simplicity into the process of living. (Dr. Steven Weinberg)

"Scientific literacy demands that we know the laws of nature. We need to inspire ourselves to know how the world works."

(Neil deGrasse Tyson)

"Scientific knowledge is the origin of our future consciousness!"

(Elon Musk)

Living Knowledge is the Origin of All Consciousness!

3. "Don't Teach Just the Subject, Teach the Whole Person!" *(Leo Vygotsky)*

Our reaction to the challenges of life that are always there should also be aware, conscious, and **the MANUAL OF LIFE** that I mention above *should be simple, inspiring, and changing in sync with its evolutionary leaps* instructing us how to live-in harmony with the Universal Laws of Nature that we keep violating for centuries on end.

I have made a modest attempt to touch on the subject in the next three books on the holistic paradigm of self-creation, *"Living Intelligence or the Art of Becoming," "Self-Taming" and "Beyond the Terrestrial!"* featuring the mental, spiritual, and universal dimension consequentially. *(See the Book Rationale)*

I have verified all my ideas many times with students that *are hungry for inspiration and the direction in life*, and I think that the role of every educators is to imbue their students with the inspiration to be fit for a new vision of life. The instruction of *Leo Vygotsky* that I mention on top of this chunk of information *is, was, and will be* my main method to follow

We desperately need the SCIENCE OF LIFE as the subject to be studied in schools and individually, *enriching the religious foundation of life with the scientific background, with due respect for both*. Both have contributed a lot for the humanity's enlightenment soul-wise.

Science is still searching for the final theory of everything, but we must be aware of its twists and turns to revolutionize the idea of who we are and where we are going. *"The increasing simplicity in the description of nature points to the fact that the final theory of everything is very beautiful and simple."* (Steven Weinberg, Nobel Prize winner) So, conscious thinking and mindful acting are of a major significance now. Other than that, the lack of emotional intelligence in us *(Daniel Goleman)* makes this task tougher. Manners are not studied at schools, and they are far from being aristocratic. There is no awareness in self-psychology.

Psychological Intelligence must not be in negligence!

No doubt, *the cultivation of the mind and the character* is needed for every one of us, worried that purity of our souls is becoming an anachronism that needs to be saved for other" *isms"-racism, nationalism, chauvinism, and moral reformism*. Not to fake the values that are in you innate, honestly declare,

I Am on the Quest for My Very Best!

4. The Grid of Our Consciousness Integration

In the Introduction to the book, I have outlined the state of our self-consciousness development and the reasons that prompt the necessity for **THE MANUAL OF LIFE** that I call upon the educators and scientists to create. Science is trying to unravel the mystery of consciousness that makes us the top of evolution at least in our universe and that helps us *put the pieces of the life puzzle* together.

"The conscious mind is ruling our evolution and is propelling the growth of our consciousness away from automatism." (Michael Ford and Peter Berkrot) *"Consciousness is the source of what we are! (Sadhguru)*

"It relates to the adulthood of our mind development" (John Baines).

The development of our self-consciousness cannot be accomplished unless we *renew our intelligence* in sync with *the Universal Laws of Creation,* and unless we expand our cognition and perception of these laws in full connection with the five dimensions of life, with the technology enhancing the reception.

The Raised Self-Consciousness propels us on-ward, up-ward, and God-ward!

Super Level	*Consciousness of God*	*Universal Dimension*
Macro Level	*Consciousness of the Universe*	*Spiritual Dimension*
Mezzo Level	*Consciousness of the World*	*Mental Dimension*
Meta level	*Consciousness of the Society*	*Emotional Dimension*
Micro Level	*Consciousness of Man*	*Physical Dimension*

The raised self-consciousness propels us on-ward, up-ward, God-ward!

We need to considerably increase our understanding of the universe, get rid of the old delusions and rewire our minds *to get out of unlit caves of consciousness.* The consciousness of both the society and the world that is presented above is being now formed by an unprecedented socialization and globalization of our lives that promote our gradual consciousness ascending.

We, in fact, develop *the holistic consciousness of inter-dependency* which is not just three-dimensional *(Hight, width, depth),* but is *four-directional* because it has **THE VOLUME** of our souls that encompasses everything around us and generates *the feeling of Oneness* inside and outside of us!

To Operate in the Universal Web Mall,

Work on the Consciousness of Your Soul!

5. The Conceptual Structure of Intelligence

In the book "***Living Intelligence or the Art of Becoming***," *the Global Excellence Book Award winning book*, which features the next*, mental* dimension of self-creation, *(See Book Rationale)*, I present **the cognitive map of mind-monitoring** that can give you a new scientific worldview, processing it holistically through five stages of self-consciousness development that, on the spiral of self-evolution, we need to raise consistently.

1) Mini - ***Physical level 2***) Meta – ***Emotional level 3***) Mezzo - ***Mental*** level
4) Macro – ***Spiritual level 5***) Super – ***Universal level***

As it is Above, in your head, so it is below, in your body!

Super Level	*Intelligence of God!*	*Universal Dimension*
Macro *Level*	*Intelligence of the Universe*	*Spiritual Dimension*
Mezzo *Level*	*Intelligence of the World*	*Mental Dimension*
Meta *level*	*Intelligence of the Society*	*Emotional Dimension*
Micro *Level*	*Intelligence of Man*	*Physical Dimension*

The Universal Intelligence is the Conceptual Structure of life!

The consciousness-intelligence of a man is part of the consciousness- intelligence of the universe. ***"Life is a spiral, not a circle."*** *(Dr. Frederick Bell),* and" ***knowledge comes from the space.***"*(Nikola Tesla) So,* the higher a person's consciousness / intelligence is the stronger and nobler his soul is. This is a given! Therefore, individual consciousness needs to be refined and developed through the process of constant enriching of intelligence, on the one hand, and committing to more heart-based, noble actions in life, on the other.

Intelligence and inner grace form the matrix of consciousness!

In sum, conscious auto-suggestive boosting, as well as continuous development of *aware attention to life and living* that helps develop *head + heart unity*, are desperately needed now because we cannot afford the luxury of automatic living anymore.

So, intellectualize your heart and emotionalize the mind!

Be One of a kind!

Processing of the Universal Intelligence Gust is the Urgent Must!

6. The Emotional Control is in the Realm of the Whole!

As is indicated above, the pressure of the present-day life demands that we prove our **intellectual exceptionality and emotional uniqueness** as universally directed and evolved beings. **Learn Emotional Diplomacy to live without impulsivity and obstinacy!** The five levels of self-consciousness development, outlined above and our mental self-creation in the spiral of ten intelligences accordingly, *(see the mental level of the holistic paradigm below)* need to be utilized in our consciously governed, more spiritualized, and holistically channeled lives.

It a true challenge because we need *to add quality to the quantity of changes*, *integrating the digital and biological realms of life*. The process of merging of the biological and digital intelligences is going on now, defined in science as the phenomenon of "*Singularity.*" Meanwhile, the level of human intelligence / consciousness is monitoring the noble side of this transformation only if a person is individually liberated, not society-indoctrinated!

"We need to transcend the idea, "My way or the highway!" (David Wilcock)*

If *the Unified Field of Consciousness (Dr. John Hagelin)* is digital and eternal, the energy of the dead people is circulating somewhere out there, channeling our actions though intuition if we are perceptive enough to attune to the information that is digitally transmitted to us. For centuries, people believed that the **dead are watching over the living!**

To unite the inner energies with the outer ones means the transformation of both, and this process requires dramatic change in our education – the change of a person in *the physical, emotional, mental, spiritual, and universal* realms of life. Becoming more holistically developed in accordance with the demands of the *"exponentially-growing technological singularity."(Ray Kurzweil),* we will become *more intuitively and telepathically connected* to each other on Earth and beyond its celestial limits. Notably, *the* freedom of speech should be supplemented by the freedom of thought in this respect.

It is vital to have freedom of thought, not just the freedom of word!

In sum, our common soul-refining needs a shift in our thinking and feeling, speaking and acting at the time of an incredible influx of digitized intelligence into the process of our conscious self-creation and self-installation.

To Self-Excel, Re-Invent Yourself in Every Cell!

7. Don't Be Soul-Contaminated; Be Soul-Elated!

Every one's intelligence, or his / her personal biological computer, is an integral part of the Universal Intelligence, or *the Master Computer, the Source* of the universe. So, the more self-developed, intelligent, and connected to the Universal Intelligence we are, the higher we can evolve on the ladder of consciousness evolution that, as science proves, is monitoring us digitally. We are all part of the whole phenomenon of life in the universe, and our interdependence demands ***we create a new operational system of education*** *with the physical, emotional, mental, spiritual, and universal* self-growth enhancement.

Every Human Contact is a Responsibility!

Every one of us must become accountable for the degradation of his /her soul that is driven by our automatism, materialization, racism, nationalism and religious dogmatism. **In the turmoil of life, we do not take care of our souls**. We twist them with lies, cheating, tongue-lashing, curses, and all kinds of compromises that generate *twinges of conscience.*

Conscience is the turning fork of the inner music of the soul!

Apparently, to universally survive, we need to get better in the physical, emotional, mental, spiritual, and universal dimensions of *the Universal School of Life.* Self-awareness and much better life awareness are essential in character -building of a person who has chosen the path of *self-resurrection* in a consciously lived school of life. Only life-aware intelligence and consciously raised self-consciousness humanize the soul. Also, we need to stop expecting people to act as we want them to. Different levels of intelligence and self-consciousness generate unsurmountable obstacles in understanding of each other. Technological enhancement should be backed up by solid self-education.

We need Living Intelligence and the Living Skills to operate Life properly.

We need to finally stop expecting people to do things that they are incapable of, like we cannot ask kids from the kindergarten to solve the tasks of the calculus. Then accusations come on the scene that are inevitably followed by justifications. *We stop caring, and become indifferent, impersonal, and soul-dead.* Such situations ruin the relationships and generate bitterness that roots inside and *de-humanizes the soul* that will have a wake-up call, anyway. That's what a great British writer *Somerset Maugham* meant when he wrote,

"The Mills of God Grind Slowly, but They Grind Exceedingly Small!"

8. Self-Education Channels Soul-Gradation!

The Universal School of Life cannot be avoided, dropped from, or disregarded. This is the education that determines our present. The one who does not correct the mistakes he made is doomed to make them again. The amount of the soul energy that is being allotted to the souls for this education is being determined by *"the Universal Bank of Consciousness" (Robert Stone)* that keeps the deposits of good deeds or becomes depleted from the withdrawals of the bad ones.

Everything is connected to everything, and our actions are being recorded!

Then, when you are ready to leave your human body, or *to graduate from the School of Life,* you'll have regrets about the uselessly spent lifetime in it, loaded with grudges and uncut Gordian knots. Degrees do not matter here; the money accumulated, or the fame accomplished do not count. As *David Wilcock* states,

"Information is transforming the very nature of our consciousness itself!"

I witness the gaps in my students' life knowledge awareness grow wider from year to year, but once I manage to inspire them with self-growth, their eyes begin to shine, their souls get nobler, their hunger for knowledge becomes insatiable. The quantity of the knowledge provided turns into their **INNER SELF-QUALITY.** They build up a much more *humanized* and *intellectually spiritualized* picture of SELF - a **NOBLE, INTUITIVE,** and **TELEPATHIC** human being. They start thinking about living more meaningful, totally self-realized lives, following the holistic paradigm: *Self-Synthesis - Self-Analysis - Self- Synthesis!* The process of <u>generalization – selection and strategizing</u> of life must be knowingly and consciously done.

Internalizing of knowledge - Personalizing it - Actualizing the dream!

In sum, the quality of the lived years is what makes a difference. The choice is yours, and it depends on the intelligence you gain and the ways you choose to use it. There are five essential qualities, **5 R's,** that we need to install in our refining souls: *be rational, responsive, respectful, reliable, and responsible.* Thus, one can stop *"the destruction of the ungodly man inside" (Peter 3:6)* and conquer the ungodly features of the inner Self that are the hurdles on the way to s*elf- awareness, self-monitoring, self-installation, self-realization, and self-salvation!* So, let's stop the dissonance of the mind and heart's farce and establish the consonance of our souls' life waltz!

The music of the heart and mind needs to be refined!

A Pure Sounding of the Soul is Our Goal!

9. Self-Perfection and the "Singularity" Reflection

The scientists claim today that *"the artificial mind will be developing its own consciousness" (Ray Kurzweil) "The future of human race does not look promising as it encompasses the accelerated development of cold inhuman intelligence without love and spiritual content."(John Baines)* This prediction by John Baines is happening right now, and the degradation of our soul qualities is obvious. With the progress of the information technology, the computers will achieve the level of human performance. **(t*he phenomenon of Singularity)*** This merging of the human brain with the technology will create a new neo-cortex in the brain, and our intelligence will become different. Our biological sameness will disappear, and we'll transcend our human capabilities. The question arises,

What about our soul qualities? Will we, machine-enhanced, retain them?

Also, what about our soul characteristics, among which **nobleness is the highest one in our definitions of human integrity**. Will robots be consciously kind, compassionate, responsive, empathetic, and considerate? I do not think that **subjective self-consciousness will be simulated**, and the future hybrids will be able to demonstrate the highest human qualities that the humanity did not obtain at mass. We keep talking about **the Golden Age** coming or **the time of Christ's Consciousness**, but the scientists predict that <u>the non-biological intelligence-consciousness will be attributed to the machine very soon, and it won't be controlled by an operator</u>. In view of this menacing change of our human essence, we need to think how to incorporate noble soul characteristics into the hybrid's thinking and how to connect it to the heart, if it remains human. Such mind will inevitably **become de-personalized.**

The technological clones will be just heartless drones!

So, our technological transformation should not be disconnected with self-evolution, that is in fact, sculpturing oneself creatively and consciously in the *physical, emotional, mental, spiritual, and universal levels of* consciousness development, presented above. The phenomenon of **the Golden Section** that is ruling the world of universal chaos and that is turning it into order, harmony, equilibrium and breath-taking beauty can hardly be programed in the machine. So, I agree with *Nikolai Roerich*, a great Russian painter, theosophist, and philosopher when he predicted,

"Only Beauty that is Consciously Perceived Will Save the World!"

10. <u>Self-Consciousness is the Soul's Spiritual Vehicle!</u>

Regrettably, it is an accepted fact that we are often driven by the automatic actions, chaotic emotional and intellectual life, and thoughtless, media-directed behavior. *"We have become "a race of human robots." (David Icke)*

Autonomy of thinking is a vital goal in refining the soul.

We are, undoubtedly, becoming more and more the race of programmed minds that think, feel, and act automatically, unconsciously, and irrationally. The vastness of the Universal Intelligence is limited by our ***intellectual laziness and stereotyped thinking*** that are booming at the technological evolution.

We grudge time needed to be spent on self-work and self-growth.

Much of life-transforming information is wasted with us in the turmoil of everyday life. Problems sweep us away, and technology is just speeding up their piling up if it is used just to automatize and robotize our life. But technology can be used to develop our intelligence, grow our consciousness, and ***purify our souls*** because ***technology is a supplementary evolutionary tool*** in our conscious time-space relationship with the world.

In the future, ***our intelligence will merge with the artificial intelligence*** and, hopefully, we will be less materialistic, more generous, and much more intelligent because technology will shoulder many of our worries. It will make a lot of problems solvable, channeling our lives along the holistic route of SYNTHESIS – ANALYSIS - SYNTHESIS for us. Meanwhile, we need to stop the chaotic style of life and try ***to intellectually synchronize this process*** in our personal lives. Information processing needs to be consciously controlled not to be buried under its snowballing avalanche.

<u>Generalization – Selection - Actualization!</u>

Only with the ***rationalization of life*** and ***conscious use of technology*** can we deal with the tribulations of life philosophically because they are an inseparable part of the entropy process that goes together with evolution. The process of knowing is endless, and it is a great honor to say, like Socrates," *I know I know nothing, the rest don't know even that!"* So, let's consciously tune to new knowledge vibrations and intelligence reformations. In our new quest for the meaning of the conceptual structure of life, <u>we are learning to decipher the digital text that is transmitted to us from the Above.</u>

"As it is Above, so it is Below!" *(The Hermetic Philosophy)*

Let's Soul-Philosophize to Become Wise!

The Soul's

Enigma

"Apply Your Heart to Instruction and Your Ears to Words of Knowledge" (Proverb 22. 12)

Don't Base Your Life on What People Think about You; Be a Self-Guru!

Souls Do Not Die!

They Relive and Thrive!

1. The Soul's Enigma Without Any Stigma

We are living at an amazing time that maximized human abilities, when on top of the most amazing discoveries and breakthroughs, we find out that science has acknowledged a seemingly impossible fact that behind everything, inside and outside of us, is *the Master Mind, or the Universal Creative Consciousness* that we all call God. Religion and science that have been in defiance for centuries appear to be the two sides of the same coin. It was proven that *the structure of the DNA, this formula of life, is identical in plants, animals, humans, and in different languages.*

Even the vibrations in the organic and non-organic objects are the same. We are probing *the science of the bio-computer of consciousness*, and we are trying to create computers, self-generating consciousness that wouldn't need any human monitoring. The enigmas of God, Soul, Spirit, and Consciousness have been probed for centuries. They have puzzled the humanity for generations, and now, with the help of the most fantastic discoveries in physics and mathematics, we are getting a new, enlightened vision of life.

"If I see, I will believe!" said a man. "If you believe, you will see!" said God.

The soul has been viewed as a sacred phenomenon in every religion. The Tora, for instance, starts with the morning prayer of *gratitude to God for having returned the soul* to the one praying. The enigma of this return is still a mystery Among many theories of the soul, the greatest ancient Greek philosophers, such as *Socrates, Plato, Augustine, and Aristotle* believed that soul was immortal and eternal.

Plato thought that the soul is a substance, a self-contained entity that temporary exists in the body and is capable of independent existence in another world. He believed in *"the treatise of the soul - reason, spirit, and appetite"* that included all the myriad of desires. Aristotle in his *"Nature of the Soul"* considered the soul to be" *the principle of life."* He thought that the soul was restricted to human beings, or conscious beings, and he even thought that *"a carrot and a dog"* could have it, too. Most importantly, *Aristotle* considered the soul *to be the element of cognition* that he called *"the rational soul."* He wrote,

"Soul is to Body as Form to Matter, as Actuality to Potentiality."

2. The Conceptual Structure of the Soul

Naturally*, the synthesis of a person's mental-emotional energy* is essential in the holistic process of consciousness raising while a person is living, and, as science holds it, *it is even more fundamental at the time of a person's death*. After we die, each soul goes beyond the terrestrial boundaries up there somewhere, being pushed up by a strong influx of mental energy into the mind of the person who had died that, in turn, pushes it back to *the Unified Field of Energy* that had generated it, to begin with. A soul is not a separate entity; it is part of the whole - *the Universal Field of Consciousness.*

Two wonderful scientists, *Dr. Stuard Hameroff and Sir Roger Penrose*, from Oxford University who are working **on the Quantum Theory of Consciousness** claim that **souls do not die!** Isn't it amazing and totally mind-blowing to finally scientifically admit it!! They call it ***"the result of Quantum Gravity Effect."***

These scientists state that the brain cells hold the soul within their internal structures, called **microtubules** *"that possibly hold the quantum information that can exist outside the body, perhaps indefinitely, as a soul"*

Souls do not die; they relive and thrive!

Trying to extend our thinking on this scientific premises, I dare assume that death is the stage of *analysis in the eternal cycle of life,* following the paradigm:

Life-Synthesis – Life- Analysis - Life- Synthesis

While a person is alive, the soul performs a unique transcendental event. *"It raises a person over his own animal instincts and achieves the manifestation and use of the higher intelligence of a human being that the evolution requires." (John Baines).*

It pushes the soul up into the digitally mental eternity.

It goes like this: a soul digitally communicates with the mind; the mind is in touch with the brain. The brain electrically is wired with the body that together constitute a person's self-consciousness - the product of the consciousness- intelligence of each cell in the body – *a man's life!* This **life-synthesis**, in its turn, is a tiny cell in *the Oneness of the Universal Mind* that governs the process of life and death on the universal scale.

"The Soul Can Do Nothing Directly;

It is You who Makes it work Through the Brain." *(Osho)*

3. Life – Death – Life Cycle

To simplify the conceptual structure of *life-death-life cycle*, let's visualize the reverse transformation of a soul. When a person dies. his body dies first, then the brain electrical circuit shuts down. The mental energy of the mind that had been accumulated by *the brain in synch with the heart* and every cell of the body during the lifetime of a diseased, pushes the soul up back into the eternity.

Add your soul's bit to the Universal Outfit!

It becomes a transformed *death–analysis entity,* meant to generate another life form and let *a new life–synthesis* manifest itself through the time and space again. Later, the released entity *synthesizes the energy for a new transformation* of a life form, continuing the never dying cycle of **life-death -life** found in everything on Earth:

Don't take Life for granted; It's God granted!

In sum, *intelligence and self-consciousness need to be developed in sync*, and this process of the incorporation of the heart and mind needs to be considerably enhanced by the exponential growth of *technology to forestall the inevitable de-personalization of the soul* that will make our individual soul-characteristics and our *heart -to-heart and soul-to- soul communication* impossible. There are zillions of sites on the Internet that have a strong *negative distinctive magnetic field.* It takes aware attention, sifted intelligence, and true wisdom to resist the destructive force, magnetizing the untrained mind and a blind soul.

Install the anti-viral soft-ware in your mind! Be One of a Kind!

To establish the future *telepathic interaction*, we need to have the ability to perform the information selection, based on holistic unity of our souls.:

Body+ Spirit+ Mind + Self-Consciousness+ Universal Consciousness

= A New, Whole Self!

If we unify our souls in this way, the question **HOW TO LIVE?** *will be changed to a much more soul-refining question* **WHY TO LIVE?**

Birth – Death – Rebirth = Eternal Life!

The Goal of Live is not Just to Survive;

It's to Create, to Love, to Give, and to Thrive!

4. Intelligence Refining is Soul-Redefining!

No doubt, a goal-oriented *self-refinement or* **SOUL RECOVERY** *(See Stage Four below)* can be more productive if this process is monitored by the blueprint of the intellectual growth in *five dimensions and ten levels of intelligence* correspondingly. The holistic development of intelligence along these lines will inevitably raise your life-awareness and self-consciousness, expanding emotional intelligence and the soul characteristics on the way.

There is no soul-growth without being wisdom engrossed!

Such **INTEGRAL** *mental-emotional self-creation* is very helpful in the seasonal soul assessment *(see below,* and it will make your self-perfection more conscious, effective, and accurate. We'll manage the truth of life better and look at things from the **MICRO** to **SUPER** levels **INCLUSIVELY.** The information presented in this book and the boosters illustrating it will inspire you to go to the new levels of self-installation with *alert awareness* and *a conscious plan of action*. *(For more, see "Living Intelligence or the Art of Becoming!* The holistic approach opens the new horizons of vision.

Ten Stages of Living Intelligence to be mastered:

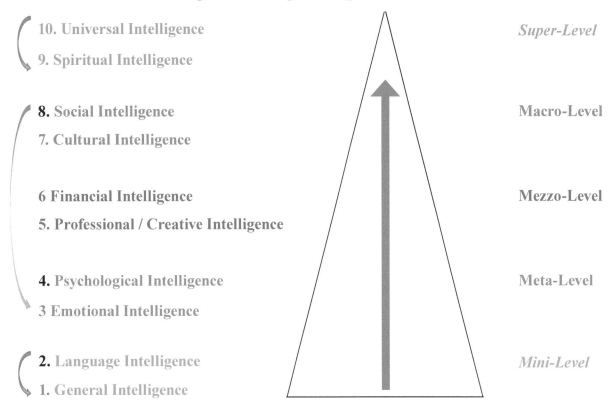

10. Universal Intelligence   *Super-Level*

9. Spiritual Intelligence

8. Social Intelligence   Macro-Level

7. Cultural Intelligence

6 Financial Intelligence   Mezzo-Level

5. Professional / Creative Intelligence

4. Psychological Intelligence   Meta-Level

3 Emotional Intelligence

2. Language Intelligence   *Mini-Level*

1. General Intelligence

We are all Life-Long Learners of the Art of Living!

5. That's the Way to Self-Find and Soul-Refine!

Obviously, the higher a person's consciousness is, the stronger and nobler his soul is! Therefore, our souls need to be refined and developed through the process of enriching our intelligence and committing to more rational, heart-based, and noble actions of giving the best we have to the world, next.

The Holistic Paradigm of Self-Resurrection:

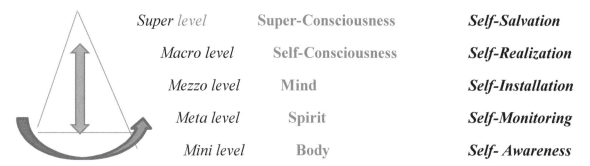

Super level	**Super-Consciousness**	***Self-Salvation***
Macro level	**Self-Consciousness**	***Self-Realization***
Mezzo level	**Mind**	***Self-Installation***
Meta level	**Spirit**	***Self-Monitoring***
Mini level	**Body**	***Self- Awareness***

The Fractal Mode of our souls:

Body+ Spirit+ Mind + Self-Consciousness+ Universal Consciousness =

New, Whole Self!

Developing knowingly and holistically, we are constructing A **NEW CONCEPTUAL CONTENT OF LIFE,** that, in my understanding, ***has a fractal structure,*** following *David Wilcock's* mesmerizing conclusions about "*a fractalized mode of the entire Universal System.*" New consciousness of the society and the world, destroying the old one and using the entropic energy that is released on this path to construct **THE NEW MEANING OF THE UNIVERSAL TEXT** that we are perceiving from the Above and constructing digitally now, connecting our two brains and activating *the Pineal Gland* in the brain that plays this integrating role. We are all ignorant on different subjects, and we need to have the holistically- fundamental vision of one, commonly shared reality. Naturally, we should be describing it from one level of consciousness to the next *in an inoperable unity with the heart,* developing *emotional intelligence in tandem with the general intelligence.*

Consciousness is the mental-emotional core of a soul; it's the soul itself!

The energy of consciousness is real energy of the soul. ***It is called psychotronic energy,*** and it is changing now. Our goal is to learn to tap into this energy with our intuition and let it channel our thinking, speaking, feeling, and acting to become ***the godly masters of life.***

Outside Information ➞ Inside Transformation!

6. Life Awareness + Self-Awareness = A Soul's Fairness!

In the first book on self-formation, *"I Am Free to Be the Best of Me, (See Book Rationale)"* I call on us to learn to be fair to life and people, developing an independent, critical perception of yourself and the life around you. I introduce **the main auto-suggestive formula** that I suggest using as your **Self-Hypnosis** to fortify self-confidence in five levels of soul- resurrection integrally.

I know who I am!

<u>I am a strong, calm, and determined owner of my firm will!</u>

I can do whatever you need; I want to …; And I will…!

Please, note that the messages that are auto-suggestively transmitted get rooted in the brain to pop up at the right time and back you up mentally and emotionally. The concepts that they are carrying are not just sentimental. <u>They are very persuasive, psychologically backed up and easily. memorable.</u>

As part of the electro-magnetic field around us, ***"we are electricity at work"*** *(Nikola Tesla),* and our hearts and minds need to be charged by the spirit. A poetic word touches the heart and charges the mind. If it is written sincerely, it is a great force of a man's soul formation. No wonder *Nikola Tesla* recited *"Faust" by Goethe* by heart when he had to solve any of his problems. He said, ***"Positive mental energy can be found in the music of Bach and Mozart and in the verses of great poets. They are our main inspiration."***

The fluctuations that are at the very core of a poetical word, as well as in classical music, literature, and art in general are the vibrating waves or strings, according to *the unifying "string theory"* in physics. These fluctuations sooth our souls, raise our self-consciousness, and help us reason out the gift of life" ***that is but an hour long."*** *(Boris Pasternak)* Beauty unifies and saves the troubled souls**.** It affects even those who have no true understanding of art and music.

The soul resonates to higher vibrations of life to thrive, not just to survive!

In the future, we'll merge with the machine through computation of our brains. We will incorporate more resources for the Universal Field of energy thanks to the effect of Singularity that has already started manifesting itself. Meanwhile, "<u>a smart phone is the brain, expanded to the cloud</u>" *(Ray Kurzweil)* that can be used as the best self-help device in re-programming of the brain.

<u>Auto-Induction is the Onto-Genesis of Self-Production!</u>

7. Beat the Self -Defeat!

In sum, a self-creation process is getting more aware of *the conceptual structure of life* in which each soul counts because it is a part of the whole - **the *Consciousness of God -*** the light at the end of the tunnel that we are heading to. One thing should be stable and unarguable in our search of that light. We need to create ourselves and uplift our consciousness every minute, hour, day, month, year, all our lives in the five dimensions*: physical, emotional, mental, spiritual, and universal.*

I am promoting the necessity to refine our souls in all these dimensions ***holistically and auto-suggestively*** because I see how inspirational word uplifts my students and friends, my readers and the loved ones. A rhyming word resonates with their hearts and minds and helps them take life in stride. With a simple blueprint of self-perfection in mind, a person gets better self-aware and life conscious.

Life is matter + intelligence or self- consciousness in motion!

The ongoing *information* ⟶ *transformation* process is a never-ending genetic formula, modifying our minds and hearts exponentially ***"at the cellular level." (****Dr. Bruce Lipton*). But only the unity of both makes our souls an extension of our eternal minds. ***Every soul has a mental-emotional energy core*** that is charged with the intelligence of its owner.

Self-consciousness is the energy of the mind and heart in sync!

Therefore, consciousness needs to be refined and developed through the process of enriching a person's intelligence and committing to more rational, heart-based and noble actions in life

Thus, we stop being impersonal and become inter-personal!

Developing intelligence in an inseparable link with the heart, we are constructing a **NEW CONCEPTUAL CONTENT OF LIFE,** *individually*, and new consciousness of the society and the world, *socially*. Destroying the old patterns of behavior, we will be using the entropic energy that is released on this path *to construct new meanings of the universal text* that we are tapping into digitally now. We will be describing it from one level of consciousness to the next in an inoperable unity with the heart.

Beat the Self Defeat with Discipline and the Unbeatable Spirit's Spin!

Let's Soul- Philosophize to Become Wise!

The Soul's Mass in Us!

(Don't Be Soul-Contaminated; Be Soul-Elated!)

Every Soul has the Choice to make –

To Be in a Self-Stagnation, Self-Degradation, or a Self-Salvation State!

Life is a Wonder Puzzle for the One

Who is Life-Dazzled!

The Spark of Each of Us is in the Soul's Mass!

The New Age Blessing is the Soul's Reassessing!

Life Itself is
the Gift of Your Cells!
They All Work in Unison
to Help You Sing
Your Swan Song!

Use technology for your Soul's Ecology!

Upload your smart phone with a new inspirational tone!

Delve into the Depth of knowledge and Keep it in the Mind's storage!

1. The Soul-Enlightened Life

Next, let me present *Aristotle's* vision of the soul. He wrote, *"There can be no soul without a body, and the main substance of the soul is **the Effie.**"* The present-day science identifies "the effie" as ***"The Unified Field of Consciousness."*** *(Dr. John Hagelin)* Dr. Hagelin presents an amazingly holistic structure of *the Unified Field* as the ***"Ocean of Pure Existence."***

We are getting a new life vision with a digital precision!

Another great physicist, *Nassim Haramein* sees the Unified Field of Information **as repeated patterns of interrelated structures**. He writes, "We *are part of this Universal Ocean of Intelligence / Consciousness."*

So, our souls are not separate entities, but inseparable parts of the whole.

Therefore, improving the soul means improving the intellectual performance of the self-consciousness that needs ***to transcend the Self to become closer to merging with Pure Intelligence / Consciousness*** at every level of our existence - *physical, emotional, mental, spiritual, and universal,* underlying our subjective and the objective visions of life, or *"**our inner and outer intelligence**"* and considerably raising life awareness with love for it, oneself and the loved ones.

Awareness is a conscious attitude to oneself, the people and life at large!

In the fractal structure of the soul, I present the trinity of the **BODY + SPIRIT + MIND**, inflated by rising self-consciousness thanks to our developing intelligence. It enriches the intuition and, therefore, generates our connection to the Pure Consciousness, the Source, or ***the Super Consciousness*** of life itself.

To conclude this third philosophical part of the book, I would like to give my most gracious thanks to all our incredible scientists, philosophers, New Age writers, and spiritual gurus that are posting their insights on line, enlightening the public, changing our belief systems, and *expanding our physical, emotional, mental, spiritual, and universal realms of life perception in the holistic unity.* People all over the planet are waking up to a new, aware mind-set - ***fractalizing their souls in the Universal way*** and developing themselves in this direction.

The Spiritual Fractals of our Refining Souls:

Form + *Content*

(Body+ Spirit+ Mind) + (Self-Consciousness + Universal Consciousness) =

Form + Content = A New Life Spiritualized Soul!

2. Human Life Without a Stigma!

(An Inspirational Booster)

Human life is an enigma

That leaves on everyone a moral stigma

> *Of petty passions and vices*
>
> *Of endless desires, garnished with sexual spices!*

This enigma, though, is movable,

And as we mature, it becomes removable!

> *But to clean up your moral set,*
>
> *You need to have a spiritual bet*

To will your power more

And to stop being a desire hoare!

> *You must seize being a human worm,*
>
> *Crawling up the hill of a twisted human form!*

You need to declare your new liberty

From the rule of money and common stupidity!

> *Then, you'll get to know the why and the when*
>
> *You can deserve your own Eden!*

You'll develop a new life menu

And commit to life in its true value!

> *You'll erase the common enigma*
>
> *And become a unique being without a stigma!*

So, try to live without a sin

Even though it seems to be obscene!

Never Lose the Sight of Your Divine Might!

3. Souls Do Not Die; They Spiritually Survive!

As it was noted above, souls go beyond the terrestrial boundaries up there somewhere because they are not separate entities. They are part of the whole – *the Unified Field of Energy* that we all came from, to begin with.

After a person's death, the soul of a diseased man is pushed up by the strong mental energy of the mind only to get back as transformed energy form later.

So, intelligence and energy, or idea and matter in sync govern this eternal process. If we try to go beyond our bad habits, conditioned, automatized thinking, our materialistic values, and other imperfections, the souls that is known to be immortal will become a holistic symbiosis of *matter (energy)* and *intelligence (idea)* that is harmoniously integrated by the Unified Information Field.

Be Soul-Connected; Disconnection is Death!

Life can never be stable and happy all over. It is meant to be based on up-down vibrations, minus and plus, order and chaos, destruction and construction, evolution and entropy, or God and devil at large. So, our polarized perception of life demands that we unify our differences, take life **AS IS,** and appreciate its happy and unhappy moments as the given.

Self-suggesting, or *self-hypnosis* appears to be much more effective than affirmations, quotes, or just interesting sayings in the most fluctuating events of life. Rhyming self-suggestive boosters also help resist mental slavery of stereotyped thinking and acting.

We must be stretching our minds against self-perpetuality of life in stride!

The negative force field needs to be resisted at every level consciously, and *self-suggestibility is the only method* that can help us make order out of chaos and make beautiful music out of ugly, soul-destructive noise.

The cacophony of the soul is its worst mole!

This book is a modest attempt *to present the methodology* by which we can inhibit our automatic thinking and the disintegration of our souls that we are trying to calm down at least with the help of meditation that needs to be consciously attuned to the Unified Field of energy. *(See the Transcendental Meditation)*

Life is an enigma, devoid of consciousness stigma!

I'm working on My Soul's Reformation Now, WOW!

4. Our Souls are One Under the Sun!

In sum, our souls are One with the Universal Consciousness of the Sun! Each soul is *the product of our general and emotional* **intelligence,** and it is a part of the Universal Intelligence. Every soul is sojourned by the mind of its owner, the energy of which pushes the soul up into the Eternity.

It goes like this: the soul, as the Universal Consciousness substance, communicates with the mind. The mind is in touch with the brain; the brain interacts with the body and in its inseparable unity a person's self-*consciousness* which is the product of this oneness. Together, they are developing as part of the Universal Consciousness that, if we follow *Dr. Kaku's vision,* has three levels of civilization development - the **Planetary, the Star Civilization, and the Galactic one.**

In fact, every level of civilization needs to follow its own Planetary, or *galactic consciousness* development to incorporate into the Universal One that, according to the latest developments in physics is *the Unified Field of Energy and Information. (Dr. John Hagelin)*

"Information is transforming the very nature of consciousness itself."

To simplify an unfathomable in its totality conceptual structure of the life-death reality, let's visualize *the reverse transformation of a soul* when a person dies. So, when a person dies. his **brain - body dies first**, then the brain itself.

The mental energy of the brain gets accumulated in the mind, and the mind pushes the soul up into the eternity that had generated it.

If a person's brain did not contain the mental energy enough to charge the mind, the mind is unable to push the soul up. The undeveloped, physically, emotionally, mentally and spiritually - polluted energy of the diseased person *is not accepted by the Pure Consciousness Field!*

Consequently, such soul stays close to the earth among the other dead souls, weak and insignificant to enrich with its mental-emotional energy the Universal Intelligence that had brought it to life, to begin with.

The correlation of our consciousness and the reality is there, but we need to attune our souls to this process consciously and consistently.

So, blow in much light into your internal soul's site!

Soul-Healing is Light Revealing!

5. Help Your Soul to Be Overly Whole!

(A Prayer of Protection)

Dear God, protect me from myself

And the evil human cells,

> *From sulkiness and gloominess,*
>
> *From silliness and mindedness,*

From despair

And lack of beware,

> *From the emotional dismay*
>
> *And the mental decay,*

From the inner hurt

And the outer exploit!

> *Protect me from getting on the automatic road,*
>
> <u>*Teach me to live in the conscious mode!*</u>

God is the Celestial Light Wrap that we need to

Inwardly Entrap!

<u>Light is Me; Light is My Philosophy!</u>

Those that Defy the Gravity of the Common – Thrive

Those Who are Inwardly Dry – Die!

6. Personal Evolution is the Soul's Revolution!

Undoubtedly, the hardest work to do is the work at oneself with an auto-suggestive back-up that is very helpful on the path of a personal evolution. Self-growth needs to be *self-monitored with expanded awareness of life and a positive self-regard* against the commonsense life conceptual guard.

One needs to become his own best-trusted ally, talking to his peculiar "**I AM**" directly and supporting it, if need be, with the *inspirational injections* and the *authoritative commands* that boost the spirit and fill it up with rationality, enthusiasm, love of life, and determination for action. if you happen to already be a perfect person, quite content with who you are, this book is not for you.

Stagnation cannot be the source of elation!

Soul-recovery how is for those who feel the demand of the present-day times *to* **DE-MATERIALIZE THEIR SOULS**, who witness our deteriorating values, impersonal attitude to each other, and indifference to the events in the world.

Our life roles are eroded by a massive disconnection of the souls.

We put the blame for our depleted, life-damaged souls on an exponential growth of the technological giant that is looming now over our personal and professional lives. We blame our emotional and mental turmoil on the rush of life, accelerated by the high-tech revolution, on the President, the government, the adversarial religion, the national characteristics of a person, or his / her skin color. Don't let prejudiced people determine how you must feel and live.

The Growth of Self-Worth is not for Human Moths!

The right time to fix a corrupted or beaten soul never comes because every time we have an urge to change ourselves and discover *the paradise within* is the right time. Uplift your spirit every minute!

The giants of spirit are the giants of consciousness!

Raised self-consciousness generate in us the desire *to create beauty and order* in ourselves and in the world. There are many of spiritual giants around you. Start seeking! *The one that seeks, finds!*

Many of Us are Not Life-Fit because We are Too Soul-Beat!

7. "It Too Shall Pass!"

To conclude my philosophical escapade, we need to be constantly aware of this <u>amazing conceptual structure of life and</u> take it in stride, being thankful for the bad and good that we get and never forgetting a valuable piece of wisdom of *King Solomon:*" ***It Too Shall Pass!*** " that he had engraved on his ring and that reminded to him about the interchangeable structure of life. As a matter of fact, all the religions of the world show the way of *soul-enlightenment by way of spiritual maturation.* Therefore, <u>reading the Torah, the Bible, the Koran or any other spiritual Manual</u>, backed up by meditation and constant self-growth spiritually and intellectually, is the process of soul-feeding and soul-healing.

But the process of such SPIRITUAL MATURATION *must be intelligence-based.* *(Stage Three below)* It must be the intelligence that is not just knowledge accumulation, but the intelligence that is devoid of the society's indoctrination. It must be critically individualized and self-growth oriented. We must be able to reason out the holy wisdom without a priest's or any one's help, ***doing our own brain / soul work consciously and consistently.***

Any sickness of the soul is the result of spiritual ignorance!

Ignorance is at the core of any disease - *physical, emotional, mental, spiritual, or universal.* <u>Managing life is managing ignorance in oneself</u> and outside, in these main life dimensions. Don't ever judge a person's preferences of the spiritual messages that he /she follows.

Spirituality is a private and self-conscious matter!

Spiritual maturation is the growth ladder of the soul and our private channeling it upward and modifying its twists and turns is the must in a soul-refining process. ***It is much more beneficial for the soul*** than any ritual or norms-imposing religious, automatic actions. It's an urgent necessity for every human soul to meditatively install the AUTO-ANTENNA for the reception of the messages from the Unified Field of Consciousness. The purpose of any meditation is to open the channel of communication with the Universal Mind. It is the energy force capable of ***de-materializing the irrational unconsciousness*** that every religion calls upon its follows to consciously battle inside to obtain the sacred truth of outside life, revealed to the enlightened ones.

Conscious Living means making Self-Consciousness manageable!

Consciousness is the Mental-Emotional Essence of the Soul; It is the Soul Itself!

(Five Stages of Soul-Refining and Self-Re-defining)

Five Dimensions

of Being

a Human Being!

(The Strategical Plan of Action)

Turn on your Mind and the Heart to One Beat!

Be physically, emotionally, mentally, spiritually,

and universally complete!

Change the Double Helix of an Animal DNA

into the Five-Dimensional "Star Man's" Display!

Let's Make Our Life from Birth the Heaven on Earth!

"There is Nothing in Life More Intimate than Spiritual Connection." *(Edgar Cayce)*

1. Live Today without Any Dismay!

"If you see the Moon,

You see the Beauty of God!

If you see the Sun,

You see the Power of God!

If you see the mirror,

You see the Best Creation of God!

We are just the tourists here,

And God is our tour guide.

He has designed our trips

And booked them for us.

Trust God and enjoy life!

Life is just a journey!

Live today and laugh every day!"

(Charlie Chaplin)

<u>"It's Not Enough to Be the Best - Be the Only!"</u>

(Steve Jobs)

2. The Manual of Life at Hand is the Soul's Magic Wand!

In our quest for the conceptual structure of life, *we are literally learning to decipher the universal digital text* that is transmitted to us from the Above. The present-day market is salivating for emotionally refined, technologically- gifted, intellectually advanced, and *holistically- informed people,* and, as the digital framework of life unfolds to us, such minds must be raised in our colleges and schools!

> "Wisdom is the skill to grasp the truth of the moment and deliver the correct outcome. *(Elliot B. Addison)*

Obviously, our kids need to study the *Art of Being and Becoming* or **THE SCIENCE OF LIFE** supplementary one at the start of their future academic lives. Look at the crowds of people that life-coaching professionals gather.

The thirst for the unanswered life questions is insatiable, and the interest in science is growing by the day. The sources in tips are all there, at our fingertips, but there is **NO MANUAL OF LIFE** in sight; no living skills are being developed in our youth, either.

We also desperately need to *scientifically enrich the religious foundation of life in our homes spiritually,* to expand the outlook of our kids beyond church boundaries. Obviously, we need more educational facilities that incorporate technology, electronic gaming and learning that is both fun, mind-expanding, and wisdom-providing. (*Check out "I Am Free to Be the Best of Me!"-the physical dimension)*

> *"Seek and you will find!"*

But kids need to know what to seek and what they might find. Both religion and science have contributed a lot to the humanity's enlightenment soul-wise, and they both are the *sides of one coin*. Both are needed for young minds as the basis of intelligence that challenges the status quo and shapes these new indigo children into *"the Star People (John Banes)* of the future. The digital information that we try to digest is enveloping us as the Universal Intelligence that is love-imbued or *heart + mind centered.*

Intellectualize Your Heart and Emotionalize the Mind! Become One of a Kind!

3. Put Your Soul's Refining into

the Evolutionary Perspective's Designing!

So far, in three parts of the book, presented above, I have focused your attention *on the philosophical aspects of soul-refinement*, trying to view this most puzzling phenomenon of our life through the prism of the latest science developments as processed through <u>my objective perception. of this subject.</u>

Below, I'm presenting the strategy of **SOUL-PERFECTION** as the illustrations of the **KNOW-HOW,** outlined above. You'll take a closer look at <u>soul-refining in five stages of life-redefining,</u> one by one - **Self-Awareness, Self-Monitoring, Self-Installation, Self-Realization, and Self-Salvation.** They are presented in a nutshell to help you focus on the main standpoints of the emotional self-creation.

1. At Stage One - **Self-Awareness,** *the physical dimension,* we learn to respect our bodies. The body talks to us in the language of intuition and pain. Listen to it and respond to its messages timely and consciously. *"Know Thyself!"*

It's hard to live with self if you do not know thyself!

Learn to be intuitively tuned to every organ and communicate with your cells while reflecting, meditating, programming them for health. Unite with your immortal soul that you need to continuously develop and enrich consciously because physical creativity is *bodily science in action*

2. At Stage Two **- Self-Monitoring,** *the emotional dimension,* we absolutely need to be emotionally equipped! Emotional diplomacy is the prerequisite for the aristocratism of any soul! Ordain it with patience, tolerance, respect and love.

Emotionalize your mind: Be One of a Kind!

Also, you cannot accomplish any soul improvement at this level without consciously *taming your tongue* and making it follow the lead of the mind, not your emotions. Language is the passport of your mind. So, *language intelligence* is the next peak to conquer! *Only the mind-governed tongue orchestrates the life's fun!*

3. At Stage Three - **Self-Installation,** *the mental dimension*, we instill in the mind again the idea that *living is a life-long learning*! Your intelligence, or **"THE SOUL'S MIND"''** (*David Wilcock*) is the basis for your self-installation in life. You can establish the connection with the Universal Mind only if you keep developing yours! Absolute mental clarity, *freedom from the "collective unconscious,"* and emotional equilibrium are needed at this level of Self-Resurrection. *People lean to the dark side because they are weak inside!*

"Poverty of the body can be cured; poverty of the mind is irreparable"

Absorb the knowledge, process it for its validity, sort out the redundant mess, and organize your mind into *the compartments of wisdoms at hand* that you can tap into at any time to solve any problem. *Listen to your intuition and the mind; be self-reliant!*

4. At Stage Four, **Self-Realization,** <u>the spiritual dimension,</u> you will help your Soul to be in God's Control! *We* take care of our soul's health that can be sustained only if we are *Godly, not godless* in the mind and the heart, in our thoughts and actions. Our spiritual, not just religious barometer should guide our inner weather and charge the mental compass of our lives. <u>So, tune your cells to accumulate the Universal Wealth!</u> Then loving and forgiving will become your living! *"Too few people recognize any connection between their wrongs due to ignorance and the troubles they cause to their souls." (Richard Wetherill)* Spirituality is not just adopting a spiritual attitude of the service to God and purifying our souls by getting rid of ruinous habits, it is also an everyday job of *"procuring that the spirit should be manifested though one's own brain." (John Baines)*

To become soul-wise, activate the mind + heart device!

At Stage Five, **Self-Salvation,** <u>the Universal dimension,</u> we are tuning ourselves to the entirety of life and living on Earth and in the space. Our universally oriented thinking and infinite life-perceiving through *conscious developing of intuition, telepathy, and mind-reading* have a long way to go, but we have already stepped on this path thanks to our electronically charged evolution. At the Universal level of self-development, we will reach our goals and set new ones, starting from the bottom of the next developmental level of the universal pyramid, in a spiral fashion all ever again. *"Life is a spiral, not a circle!" (Fred Bell)* You should remember, though, that <u>you can never duplicate anyone's success at self-taming or soul-refining.</u> It's your personal, deeply individualized business with its unique know-how, its actualization and realization. I like all the books on character-building by *Antony Robins*, who writes, *"If you want to be successful in life, one word is important - Progress!"*

I'm Working on My Soul's Reformation Now - WOW!

Soul's

Sojourn

A good <u>Body + Spirit+ Mind</u> outfit
makes your soul more life-fit!

"The compulsive nature of a man can be gotten rid of only thanks to
<u>*his rising self-consciousness*</u>*"*
(Anton Chekov)

Every Soul is Sojourned by the Mind of Its Owner!

I Know Who I Am!

"Life is like Riding a Bicycle.

To Keep Your Balance, you must Keep Moving."

(Albert Einstein)

1. The Soul's Health is My Main Wealth!

My bio-state is always
Great;
I never ask for energy
rebate!

Nor do I ever yell or
Frown;
I slow up my slow
Down!

Don't be limited by the wishes of the body!
Be Soul-Embodied!

"We are all Electricity, or Light, in Human Form!"
(Nikola Tesla)

2. I Am a Homo Sapience!

I am a homo sapience, but I still belong

<u>*To the animal kingdom!*</u>

> *God commands," Know thyself!"*
>
> *But I hide into my stereotyped shell!*

I know so much, but understand so little;

I am a phantom in the world of litter!

> *I get lost in the collective mind*
>
> *Of the totally blind!*

I try to rise from my own ashes, as the bird Phoenix,

But I fall into the trap of my authentic phonies.

> *"An eye for an eye" and "tooth for a tooth"*
>
> *Remain in action as the truth!*

To acquire the human quality,

<u>*Do we need a 2000-year warranty?*</u>

> *Do we have to undergo the stage of crucifixion?*
>
> *When will we stop taking Christ's story as a fiction?*

True, mal attitudes remain

In the anti-Christ domain

> *And each one needs to stop being a victim*
>
> *Of a collective dictum!*

There is one solution

In the human evolution -

To Stop Being a Homo-Sapience and

<u>Convert into a Stellar Man, Hence</u>!

3. The Evolution of My Soul

When I was born,

<u>*I was given the soul's form!*</u>

It descended with the wisdom of code,

Accumulated by it for the centuries of life's mold!

I started to unwind

Its universal mind.

I've been learning to rejoice,

To wonder and to hear the voice

Of the Creator

That is every soul's rater!

I have finally realized

<u>**That I am far from being wise!**</u>

I know that I adhere

Only to what I see and hear!

My spiritual receptors are clogged

By the ignorance of the Gordian Knot

That I cannot cut,

Without obtaining a strong personal gut!

So, to run wisely my soul,

<u>**I must put the heart and mind in control!**</u>

With the Soul, full of Spiritual Glee,
<u>I'M FREE TO BE THE BEST OF ME!</u>

4. <u>Step One - Create Order in Yourself!</u>

In the Physical Dimension of life, the level of **SELF-AWARENESS** in the holistic paradigm, our primary goal is to know ourselves. *"The better we know ourselves, the less we fear. because we are wired to be extraordinary." (Gregg Braden)"* We are driven by evolution and entropy, order or chaos, but a man creates himself by way of <u>putting his life in order</u> and directing himself through new levels of mental and emotional refinement

Self- Construction may be successful if it is based on the blueprint in the mind that demands self-awareness and much more knowledge of life. Luckily, science-based knowledge becomes the essence of goodness because by ***creating ourselves knowingly,*** we get rid of the bad self-destructive habits. Refining the soul means destroying the habit of reacting to any unpleasant occurrence in life negatively, without giving oneself time to think about the causes of the consequences of the undertaken action. chaos is ruling the soul! In his wonderful book, ***"Destiny of the Soul"***, Michael Newton writes**,** *"Everyone's soul energy must learn to balance itself within a physical body."* Reacting to any irritating signal positively, you will stop blaming, accusing, cursing, and tongue lashing. There will be no distortion of the reality that generates chaos in the mind.

<u>Praying is soul-saving when there's conscious mind-prevailing!</u>

Therefore, the behavior of an erratic person needs **SELF-REFLECTION** and at least a quick overall analysis *in a physical, emotional, mental, spiritual, and universal realms of life* <u>every day, if not every minute.</u>

Self-scanning must become a second - nature with us, thus!

Self-scanning must be based on solid self-awareness, and it needs to be ***objective***, not subjective in its core. No one knows what you are like better than you and taking criticism from oneself is less painful than from anyone else. But your judgement should be devoid of any self-pity and blind justification. That's why calming down is essential, and praying is so helpful!

Praying should be the first reaction to any mishap, not the last hope!

If we are working on self-change consciously and continuously, ***we are developing higher self-consciousness*** and, thus, ***creating order in life***. Dalai Lama's piece of advice is instrumental here,

"The Only Way is to Go Up into God and Down into Yourself."

5. Self-Destruction is Evil - Not Civil!

Naturally, order calms us down, puts everything in place in the mind, helps us think rationally, and it teaches us **emotional diplomacy**. No wonder, women start putting things in order and cleaning the rooms when they are nervous. ***Order is generating goodness, peace, and love***. We cannot eliminate evil altogether because it is part of the divine plan that constitutes unity by creating polarity. It is the balance between the two opposites that we should be seeking in life at the time that we call ***Self-Enlightenment***.

To beautify your soul, become overly whole!

Being happy, therefore, is being well-organized, balanced, self-content, moral, noble, honest, emotionally reserved and proactive. Being unhappy is being mentally and emotionally chaotic, discontent, immoral, and dishonest.

Disorder multiples evil and increases the soul's upheaval!

There is another side of the coin here. We have a new situation when technology has a potential power to destroy us through gene sequencing. We can reconstruct life itself! ***We need to hold ourselves accountable for life and self-reformation.*** So, to create oneself is to live holistically and consciously at *the physical, emotional, mental, spiritual, and universal levels*. Then, we will be able to help the world grow from ***the micro level of consciousness in each one of us to the higher level of consciousness***, destroying the old levels and creating the new ones through evolving awareness.

Keep your relationships; do not keep just good memories!

Note please, that to heal the body, ***you need to go beyond the body!*** Inducting yourself auto-suggestively, you are helping yourself to boost your spirit and become more rational *in your outside* life. Meditating, you are getting more equilibrium *from the inside,* **connecting your self-awareness to the Unified Field of mental energy** that is guarding us when we are truly attuned to it.

Fix your Auto-Antenna beam to the Conscious Universal Scene!

Take your attention to the invisible field of nothing, *"experiencing Pure Consciousness"(Dr. Hamelin)* and integrating the inner and outside worlds of life consciously. Try *the Transcendental Meditation*. It's truly soul forming!

Any problematic relation can be solved in meditation!

To Be Always Right, Be Soul-Bright!

6. Tame Yourself in Every Realm!

Naturally, more *emotionally refined, informed, and intelligence-advanced people* are always more successful in self-realization. It is also very beneficial for the society. The international relationships and the global market are suffocating without such intelligent, noble, and self-tamed people.

The more God you have inside, the more happiness you will have outside!

Quoting a wonderful book" *Taming the Chaos*" by *Rev. P. S. Berg*, we need to concentrate our will power on governing the three main aspects of a human's reformation of a soul – **MIND + HEART + SEX.** These are the three beasts that we need to tame because they constitute <u>the sacred unity of **999** and destroy the evil **666** links</u> of these fundamental driving forces of life. *(Rev P.S. Berg).*They constitute order and chaos, evolution and entropy, construction and destruction, life and death.

To beat the evil in the bud give it a strong boot in the butt!

We know that discipline, self-assessment, and self-reflection are the irreplaceable tools in the evolution of a human soul. Presently, *the intellectual cooking backed up by technology*, needs our sorting out of the ingredients that are used for such cooking by our souls. That's why **AWARE ATTENTION** must be paid <u>to the outcome product of our thinking, speaking, feeling, and acting</u> with a new sense of responsibility, whether it is a face-to face or a digital interaction that are both mediated by the heart.

<u>Make your heart smart and the mind kind! Be One of a Kind!</u>

Obviously, our kids need to study the *Art of Being and Becoming* or *the Science of Life* as one of the most essential subjects in school. Look at the crowds of people that life-coaching professionals, the most advanced scientists, and spiritual gurus gather. The interest in spirituality and science is growing by the day, and the sources are all there, at our fingertips. To get them is not a problem, but *to consciously process them is a challenge* that requires the skills of burning of the negative emotional wire in the violet spiritual fire. To become more spiritually intelligent, self-aware, and self-conscious, we need to be better informed of the reality and *perform constant self-reflecting* on the consequences of our thoughts, words, feelings, and actions. This is **THE BASIC LIVING SKILL** that needs to be consciously developed at each level. *(See the Book "Self-Taming!" - spiritual level)*

Self-Knowledge is the Origin of Self-Consciousness!

7. Connect the Mind and the Heart; Be Smart!

The soul-refining at the physical level also demands we *"vacuum our brains"* *("Scientific American, "July 2915,* or do a good *mental "house-cleaning"* to break free from the old, stereotyped patterns of thinking that had been programmed by the society, a family, and mass media. We want to set a new, free *mind-to-mind communication.* One of the reasons we often have to deal with ignorance that, according to Einstein is *"the worst enemy of the humanity,"* lies in the fact that ignorant people lack intelligence due to their *inflated thinking blindness* that is never questioned or destroyed with new consciously processed knowledge that technology provides us with.

Self-creation is the way to battle stereotyped thinking inflation!

I am calling on us here to start looking at life *as a digital phenomenon* and accept the fact that we are part of the Universal Master Mind, or" *the Unified Field of Pure Consciousness.* To decipher its messages, we need more self-education and self-modification.

"Those that have eyes, see; those that have ears hear."

As science has it, our brains are biological computers, and we need *to upload them with new programs* that reflect the time we live in and that have staggering implications for our new understanding of the universe. "As it is Above, so it is Below!" *(The Hermetic principle)*

We need to live in balance with all that God had installed!

*The Digital Intelligence (See the book "Living Intelligence or the Art of Becoming!") i*s enveloping us everywhere, and it is governing us though self-evolution as the particles in the Universal entirety, without considering our age, race, country, culture, or a religious affiliation. *Dr. Frederick Bell* in his great book *"Death of Ignorance"* writes,

"The body is the expression of our thoughts, not the race!"

A new demand of our time *is mind-to-mind and heart-to-heart* communication that needs *aware attention*, the attention that is backed up with carefully sorted-out knowledge and is channeled by life awareness. We can tap *the Informational Field or the Super Conscious Mind* for ideas and inspiration, and the necessity to develop such new *holistic, intellectual - emotional ability* becomes more and more demanding and truly captivating.

"Our Human Potential is Exponential!" *(Ray Kurzweil)*

8. <u>Self-Discipline is On the Scene!</u>

Undoubtedly*, chaos and order in their global expulsion are shaping our evolutionary function!* Our developing self-consciousness is inseparable with intelligence that needs to be processed through *ten vistas of intelligence*, (*See Part Two*) and in five dimensions: *physical, emotional, mental, spiritual, universal.* It needs constant self-scanning and *sifting of the redundant stuff!*

For something to appear, it must disappear somewhere, and if this somewhere is you, your duty is to start *a new self-construction site* with the blueprint of self-perfection in mind. Such discipline-imposed life rewards us with enriched self-content and an amazing feeling of <u>willful self-regulation</u>.

Let nothing rot in your inner store - Will your life more!

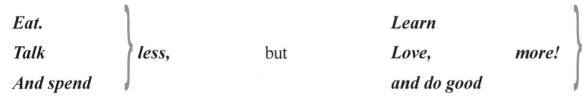

Eat.			*Learn*	
Talk	*less,*	but	*Love,*	*more!*
And spend			*and do good*	

Less is More! That's Our Physical Law!

It is an accepted fact that with *consciously observed self-discipline,* we start to enjoy life **AS IS,** without comparing it to some else's and labelling oneself as a loser. Self-discipline establishes order in every aspect of life in contrast with the chaos that destroys us and pollutes our lives in every department. **THE LIVING SKILLS** are the self-managing skills!

Chaotic Life Mismanagement

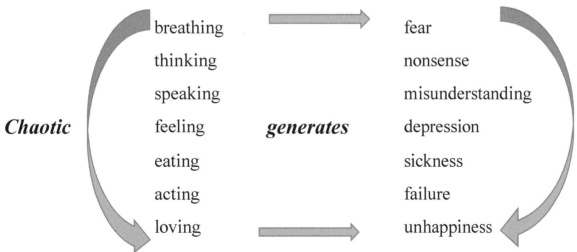

Chaotic	breathing		fear
	thinking		nonsense
	speaking		misunderstanding
	feeling	*generates*	depression
	eating		sickness
	acting		failure
	loving		unhappiness

To Perform the Evil-Rebuff, observe the rule:

"<u>Enough is Enough!</u>"

9. Clean Your Inner Oasis!

Self-scanning in the physical dimension means a self-monitored soul hygiene being conducted with aware attention, a lot of will-power, and much more understanding of self. *Magnetize, do not demagnetize your soul and its size*! Be soul and body aware!

Observe Eight Rules of Consciousness Hygiene!

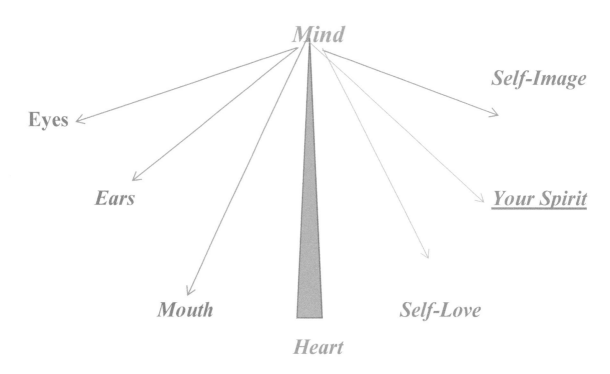

The Synergy of the day-to day Self- Hygiene is on the scene!

Your life will have a different quality, depending on the level of your life awareness - your self- consciousness - *the unity of your heart and mind*. You will gradually develop a very good habit to review your inner self for its hygiene before you go to bed, or in the morning, in the same way as you take care of your exterior. Every day, before going to work, shake off the old, dry leaves from your" *Tree of Life"*, and let it grow new, spring leaves - strong, fresh, and green.

The simplest thing in existence is to be yourself in every cell!

Beautify your thoughts, words, and needs and deeds! Learn to be aware of every moment of thinking, speaking, seeing, feeling, and acting. Enjoy your living, being, and becoming! Rejoice at soul-refining!

Getting to know thyself, you are getting to know the God's spell!

Don't Be a Human "Reptilia," Face Life with Super Criteria!

10. Observe Your Soul's Hygiene!

To have energy, we need to generate energy and learn ***to charge our souls from the Universe,*** *the Mother Nature, the Sun, the Moon, the Four Elements of Nature, from the spirit, the mind and the food we eat.* Manage your life beyond survive! ***"Men do not live by bread alone!"***

"We develop only when we train! (Aristotle).

1. Protect your mind! Delete your bad thoughts and unclutter the feelings. Use a lot of auto-suggestive injections to be always brain sharp.

Don't assume the negative thought - perfume!

2. Protect your mouth*!* Mean what you say and say what you mean!!

Foul words are language sanity warts!

3. Protect your body! Never harm or pollute your body! Do not destroy the inner rhythm of the body, its harmonious music of health. See who you let into it!

Clean it and nourish it to be life-fit!

4. Protect your heart! Make your mind kind and your heart smart! Deny yourself the luxury to react, be on a control response track!

Learn the art of seeing with your heart!

5. Protect your eyes! Clean your sight from envy, lust, and ugliness.

Eyes are the mirrors of the soul and self-console!

6. Protect your ears! Don't let gossip, foul language, and bad stories destroy your inner harmony. ***"All comes to the sound of life."*** *(Sacred Geometry)*

7. Protect your Self-Image! Love yourself first to be able to love others!

Avoid a comparison trap; be in a unique yourself wrap!

8. Protect your spirit! Don't be a low pole, a mope, or a sad sack!

9. Protect your Soul! Don't put a long face on your soul's interface!

10. Protect the time of your life! Be constantly conscious and alive!

Such integration needs constant ***self- managing or self-monitoring*** when you do not need anyone to complete your life. You feel complete, self-reliant, and self-sufficient. Go beyond the common "I survive"! Be the boss of your life!

My Intuition is the Inner Wisdom's Fruition!

11. My New Life Paradigm

I have a beautiful smile
And a sense of style,

       But I need to change the paradigm
       Of the poignant lifestyle of mine!

I communicate with God
Through the spirit's volt,

       But I need to connect the wire
       To the mind and heart of mine!

I need to learn to be right
With my spiritual might!

       For my spirit can be broken,
       If I am not outspoken!

The external forces
Often become my bosses!

       But my reaction to their function
       Is now full of repulsion!

I am not conditioned by their standards;
I have my own in abundance!

       I take charge of my life's course;
       I've put it in reverse!

As People Think in Their Hearts, so They Are!"

(King Solomon)

Emotional Diplomacy vs. the Soul's Obstinacy!

"We have a job on this planet – to learn to love and do service to others. Love is written into our Genetic Code!"

(David Wilcock)

Love and Kindness, as a Goal, Must Determine the <u>Emotional Fitness of Your Soul!</u>

Let's Beautify Our Lives with Love Lights!

The Soul's Trajectory of Love is Its
Main Emotional Stuff!

1. The Soul's Trajectory of Love

(An Inspirational Booster)

To be emotionally wise,

Incentivize yourself and the unwise!

Inject your spirit into all those

That maximize their effort only for a pose!

Imbue them with the zest to feast

Upon their depressive beast!

It'll make them forget

What evil can beget,

And it'll help them rewind

The unmanageable mind

Back to its blissful state

<u>That has been within them innate!</u>

Then, a smile starts to shine

In just a little while,

And life will get released

Without a self-pity twist!

So, if you're willing to clean your soul's dealings,

Uplift your thoughts and feelings,

Unite your heart and the mind,

<u>And Be One of a Kind!</u>

Normalcy is the product of Intelligence and Emotional Diplomacy!

2. Our Present-Day Emotional - Mental State

To come closer to the point, let me remind you that are two main personalities in each of us – *a thinking personality* and *an emotional one.* Unfortunately, they are not in sync because we lack "*emotional intelligence*" *(Daniel Goldman),* the intelligence that needs to be developed by us to manage our uncontrolled emotions and get on with developing our intelligence.

Our emotional make-up is above our mental one **yet,** and there is little, if at all, awareness how to accomplish real empowerment of emotions that have helped us survive for centuries thanks to their reactive nature. Now *emotional chaos reigns in our minds,* and unless we conquer it with our <u>well-organized intelligence in sync with new, technologically enhanced self-awareness,</u> no transformation of self-consciousness at any level will occur. "*The biology of consciousness offers a sounder basis for morality than the unprovable dogma of an immortal soul. Once we realize that* **our own consciousness is a product of our brains**, *it becomes impossible to deny our common capacity to evolve them.*" *(Scientific American Mind", July/ Aug. 29014)*

Undoubtedly, we will accomplish a new level of consciousness when *the cone of intellect will get above the cone of emotions* and **THE RATIONALIZATION** of our lives will become possible. It is going one now, but it needs to be enhanced.

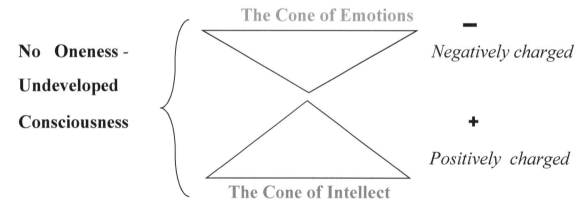

Getting into n the mental-emotional state will change your fate!

Make Your Heart Smart, and the Mind Kind! Be kind to the Unkind! Be One of a Kind!

<u>Love is a soul-to-soul connection!</u>

Make Emotional Self Discipline Your Main Gene!

3. To Self-Monitor Your Emotional Phone, Have a Self-Control Bone!

In the second, Emotional Dimension, each one of us is responsible for his / her emotional **SELF- MONITORING**. It is the basic concept of this book that aims at soul-refining in the emotional level of the Holistic Paradigm!

Self-monitoring discipline is on our life's scene!

As per the chart above (*See Book Rationale),* we need to widen our outlook exponentially by enriching our intelligence at every of *the five levels of consciousness development*, bringing the self-consciousness closer to the Universal Level. If each of us climbs **the ladder of a heart-linked intelligence**, we'll be done with ignorance and negligence!

Will your love more; that's the Law!

But one thing needs to be remembered here. The entropy of life generates chaos in our souls due *to the lack of individualized and personalized frame of thought,* and most of all, due to the ignorant automatic living. The science of life demands that **we accelerate the pace of our conscious learning** and start interpreting life in its unfathomable entirety of all the level *inclusively!*

Each of us has his / her own unique path in life that requires independent, free thinking, unconditioned by the common wisdom and the society's programming that push us to having quick, ready-made stereotyped decisions and making wrong, conditioned choices. It becomes an achievable goal if "**the right amount of effort is used in the right direction**" (*Ray Kurzweil),* and we use technology *to exponentially enrich our cognition.* In other words, we need to think, feel, and act for ourselves, without anyone's destructive interference because no one can think, feel, and do what you are able to for yourself. That's the only way on the path of transformation of <u>conditioned intelligence into super-intelligence</u> that is supposed to govern our yet untrained emotions. As *Elon Musk* puts it,

"The appearance of super-intelligence is detrimental for the humanity!"

For something to appear, it must disappear somewhere", and if this somewhere is you and your eternal soul, your duty is to start a new **SELF-CONSTRUCTION SITE** with the help of a blueprint of self-perfection. It can be done by way of developing consciousness through **ten levels of intelligence**, presented in *Part Two* and with the mesmerizing help of technology.

To Be Interesting, One Must Get Interested!

4. To Soul-Rewind, Be Kind to the Unkind!

Obviously, working at a conscious, informed, and committed *soul refining* requires a lot of self-discipline, will-power, and self-limitation. Such discipline-imposed life rewards us with an amazing feeling of self-uplifting over all the troubles and tribulations of life. *We start practicing self-restriction, devoid of self-conviction, self-justification, and blaming another.*

Love is based on intelligence, and its seat is the brain!

It is an accepted fact that with *self-discipline and a conscious emotional control,* we start to enjoy life **AS IS,** without comparing it to some else's and labelling ourselves as losers. The vastness of knowledge to be obtained and the accomplishments that our enriched and operative intelligence can produce are mind-boggling. With it, we are becoming wiser, more tolerant and love imbued. There is no self-discipline without the emotional self-control. The hardest to master is the *ability not to hit back the offender and forgive him / her afterwards*, remembering that you are not perfect, either.

The ripping effect of kindness is never mindless!

Also, there is nothing more calming and balancing than the feeling of self-worth and self-reconstruction. The auto-suggestive boosters and mind-sets are positioned in abundance in this book, presenting the stages of the holistic self-resurrection - *Self-Awareness – Self-Monitoring – Self-Installation - Self-Realization – Self-Salvation* integrally in their value for the development of EMOTIONAL DIPLOMACY that is resisting our sub-conscious obstinacy.

If you monitor your self-growth along these stages consciously, you will manage *to integrate yourself into a whole being with a strong personal integrity core.* You will become kind to the unkind, compassionate, and reserved. The most destructive mind-set" *I don't care*! would be ousted from the soul. Self- monitoring in the physical - emotional domains will become naturally integrating.

So, upload some character- making inspirational mind-sets against upsets and inspire yourself with them *willingly, willfully, and consistently.* Download a few to your smart phone, change them as needed, and have them installed in the front lobes of your brain. *They will pop up at the right time*, helping you boost your spirit that may be sagging sometimes. Auto-inductions will charge the brain with a new *mental-emotional energy* of the integrating quality.

Intellectualize Your Heart and Emotionalize the Mind! Be One of a Kind!

5. The Trajectory of True Love

The short cuts to such inner integrity are in *re-educating of our souls.* As far as true love is concerned, I share the common opinion,

The trajectory of true love is governed from the Above!

We often hear people declare that *God put them together*, that they are looking for a soulmate to finally find the One and the Only. But nothing happens for free. What have you done to become the One and the Only?

You have not magnetized your soul to attract the One for that goal!

In the holistic framework of soul-refining that I am advocating for in all my books, *true love develops from the top of the evolutionary pyramid, from the Universal Level* of our appreciation of life in the universal context first.

You get the Love from the Above blessing, if there is no fun love obsessing!

Next, love gets further inflated with *the spiritual (not just religious) identity* and mutual recognition of each other's spiritual values at the *Spiritual Level.*

To become a love dove, spiritualize your love!

When we click on these two levels, we also process love through *the Mental Level* of shared intellectual interests and goals. *To be interesting, get interested!*

Our love goal is also the mental fitness of the soul!

Finally, a romantic *emotional palette* gets gradually *love-charged*, and finally, we arrive at the *physical fusion* in the passionate unity of blossoming love of mutual respect, ripe feelings, intelligence, honesty, and insightful spirituality.

SPIRITUAL FRACTALS of THE SOULS' S LOVE – SYMMETRY:

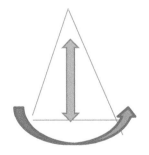

Universal Level	**Oneness** (*Inner unity with all life*)
Spiritual level	**Grace** (*Conscious faith, nobleness*)
Mental level	**Mind** (*love, based on spiritualized intelligence*)
Emotional level	**Spirit** (*will-power, commitment in love*)
Physical level	**Body** (*body-awareness*, e*nergy of love sharing*)

(Body+ Spirit+ Mind) + (Self-Consciousness+ Universal Consciousness)

The Physical Form + the Spiritual Content = True Love!

6. The Choices We Make Dictate the Life we Live!

The mind-set above is becoming critical in choosing the partner in life because your life will depend on this choice. The right choice depends on the values, instilled in your soul and *your determination to follow them in your search.* These values must be instilled in families and schools sacredly, on the basis of science-based information, backed up with the masterpieces of literature, art, and classic music and developing the **SELF-MONITORED LIFE** and the **LOVE SKILLS**. The Love Skills need to be taught and brain- trained.

Science proves that the seat of love is in the brain, not the heart!

Naturally, teachers need to be holistically developed with the background scientific knowledge that is not just tested in an administrative, dry, red-tape installed fashion, but is based on *actual life-awareness*, stimulated by self-education and self-growth. Spirituality takes a whole new meaning in this context.

It beautifies the soul and makes it whole!

Obviously, when we *click with our students intellectually and spiritually*, we *support their aspirations for true love and happiness in life.* Then, when they we get emotionally entangled and romantically enflamed, they have *the intellectual wisdom and emotional immunity* to forestall cheap, dirty sex-oriented mentality that is ruling the minds of our kids from middle school. Unfortunately, *a lot of excellent, knowledge-inspiring teachers leave schools because their aspirations are not shared by the administration.*

To develop a strong personal magnetism and respect for love, we need to remove the dead education stuff!

There will be no one nightstands, inconsiderate relationships, cruel divorces, and damaged souls. We will learn *to adorn our feelings, respect the bodies, and we stop counting innumerable soul bruises*, caused by lack of morals, ignorance, and absence of science -backed up self-awareness.

Left Brain + Right Brain keep your life Sane!

It is becoming increasingly clear that we need *to tame the old patterns of our perception of the reality and the response to it* because they are in the way of our universal evolution that needs *conscious selection of the information processed under the guidance knowingly.* I am sure that the universal role of the technological revolution is to up-grade our thinking abilities and *synchronize our brains with the self-tamed emotions.*

Put the Left and the Right brains in Sync - Feel but Think!

7. Love Normalcy is the Product of Intelligence and Emotional Diplomacy!

Apparently, the present-day education needs *to be holistically- individualized* and *personality development - focused* with a great accent put on self-education and *intellectual integrity* that is the product of both hemispheres of the brain.

The Internet is not just gaming; It's also Self-Learning and Self-Taming!

If our kids and young people study *the Art of Living and Becoming* by the best examples of the world masterpieces of love, if we stop blurring their developing souls with *violent games, dirty, immoral shows, full of profanity, fights and awful manners, t*heir everyday reflections on love for each other, the Mother Nature, and the loved ones, will be radiant and gratifying.

Being impersonal makes a soul's degradation irreversible!

The short cuts to such inner integrity are in <u>re-educating of our brains</u> and <u>reprogramming our cells</u>. *(Dr. Bruce Lipton)*, putting an accent on accentuating the **HOLISTIC PERSONALITY DEVELOPMENT**. The route of such self-installation in more detail is presented at the physical level of the holistic paradigm of self-creation in the book *"I Am Free to Be the Best of Me!*

Self- Synthesis- Self-Analysis- Self-Synthesis!

Our present trend toward loading the left-brained forces mostly *on professional specialization* with much redundant information instilled in the brain has reached the point of diminishing returns. It is becoming increasingly clear for educators that it *is vital for each hemisphere of the brain to be trained for which it is best suited! (See the book "Beyond the Terrestrial!"-spiritual level)*

<u>Soul-Reformation is based on Self-Education!</u>

"The most important thing in self-reformation is to set order in your soul. Follow the three rules – don't complain, don't blame, and don't justify yourself!" (Bernard Show)

Knowledge Needs a Lot of Linking to Generate <u>Holistically Trained Thinking!</u>

8. The Auto-Suggestive Inspirational Hygiene Must Always Be on the Scene!

Let's Create the Space of *Love* *from the Above!*

The Soul's Elation is in the *Divine Love's Inspiration!*

(See The book "Love Ecology, 2020 /www.language-fitness.com)

Women love men for their exceptionality, *men love women for seeing it in them!*

So, for a high spiritual volt, *to be not emotionally involved is* <u>*a poor soul's thought!*</u>

(Upload your smart phone with a love-sustaining tone!)

Don't Start a Relationship for a Wrong Reason; It's a Self-Treason!

9. The State of Love

(An Inspirational Booster)

To delete the messy soul stuff,

Let's create the State of Love!

      The best quality of a love-dove

      Is a constant state of love!

This state must be instilled in us, too,

And this is the love we need to look forward to!

      The sense of life is in this state;

      It is the calling of each fate!

No meditation or any mantras

Can install the love implanters!

      So, for a spiritual growth,

      Be constantly in search of a love pose!

Stop the undercurrent emotional disease

And eliminate the love freeze!

Be emotionally-still and set your expectations at this mind-set's feel!

I can…,

I want to…,

And I will…!

(For more on the main self-induction see the book "I am Free to Be the Best of Me!")

Since the Most Important Organ of Love is the Brain,

Charge with It Your Every Vein!

10. Stop the Ruling of Lust at Last!

(An Inspirational Booster)

I coax my daughter, as all moms do,

To end her endless emotional ado!

> *"To turn love into a marital bliss"*
>
> *Love the one you are with!"*

"Mom," she retorts,

Breaking the train of my thoughts,

> *"There is no love; it's only lust*
>
> *That takes the grips on us so fast!*

When you are in the USA

It's a one-night stand that has its say!"

> *True, it's hard to tell today*
>
> *Which is love or lust, per say.*

The evils of a one-night stand

Ruin the love castles sand!

> *Love goes down the drain*
>
> *In our instant gratification brain!*

The hopes and stomach butterflies

Have the life span of daily flies!

> *Marriage lasts, but a little while;*
>
> *It even stars with a sarcastic devil's smile!*

It's the money force

That rules any love's worth!

Being loaded

Is what makes love molded!

Without a solid financial stand

You've got love with no refund!

The cancer of such love value

Spreads with the speed of the mildew

Is there any review on how to turn love mildew

Into pure love-lasting dew?

We need love that reflects the sunrise of passion

And the sunset of compassion,

That has much understanding

And no mutual respect withstanding;

We need love that forms

Inspires and transforms!

But such love has to be taught and learnt;

It must be reinstalled in the young generation's fort!

And since it's in everyone's gene,

It should also be released on the social scene!

So, Let's Love by the Moral Code;
Love is Our Spiritual Mold!

11. Be in a Hurry to Understand

(An Inspirational Booster)

Be in a hurry to understand

Before being understood in your stand!

>*It's the basis for any relationship*

>*That you might worship.*

When you yell and don't hear,

You will smear

>*With an emotional haze*

>*Your high - tide love base!*

And you might turn it into a reverse --

An unpredictable storm force!

>*Untamed anger is insanity,*

>*Brewed up on selfishness and vanity!*

It ruins and destructs

The love trust acts!

>-----------------------

>*But if you shut up and listen*

>*To the other's pain in a whistle,*

If you get into his / her shoes

And perceive their emotional muse,

>*Even if their shoes are too tight*

>*For your mental might,*

You'll have the benefit of a reward

That will bring you to a desired retort -

"Yes, you are right

In your sight,

> *And I wish I could always belong*
> *To our mutual love bone."*

Thus, your love tone

Will get a new energy phone!

> *You'll become calm and loving again,*
> *And you'll restore the romance in your love stem!*

Humility resolves self-righteousness,

Admiration resolves disappointment,

Gratitude resolves resentment,

And remorse resolves hurt.

Say "Adieu!" to the Endless Love Ado!

Don't get into the Common Love Swings,

Give your love Spiritual Wings!

The Philosophy of "Immediate Gratification" is too Shallow for a Great Nation!

12. Let's Create the Space of Love!

(An Inspirational Booster)

To be happy and to never get a love rebuff,

<u>*Let's create the space of mutual love!*</u>

The center of love has a rating

That starts in the heart at its mating

With yourself, the loved ones, and the time of fun,

As well as everything under the Sun!

It's the love for your job and a true self-realization;

That's God's work in love 's gradual formation!

Your center of love gets charged,

Gradually, wholly, and at large!

Thus, Love Consciousness emotional release

<u>*Will becomes the Mind's Breeze!*</u>

The More Love You Create, the Better is Your Fate!

<u>4</u>To Be Always in a Good Mood, Make Love Your Spiritual Food!

13. My Happy Life Portion is Love and Devotion!

(An Inspirational Booster)

My happy life portions

Are love and devotion!

With love, I can rewind

Any program in my treacherous mind!

I can send love to my enemies and "frenemies,"

And I can turn them all into my admirers!

With love's blessing,

<u>My life troubles are recessing!</u>

I don't develop the dyslexia

Of the immoral love signs "reflexia!"

Thus, my mind starts monitoring the heart,

And I become very good at that!

----

*"The more routine behavior becomes, the less we are aware of it.
We lose the alert surveillance of that behavior."*

(Scientific American, June, 2014)

Fragile souls need delicate handling!

Auto-Induction:

To Succeed in the Love Bizz, Love the One
You Are with!

14. Preserve Your Inner Symphony's Surf!

An Inspirational Booster)

Being unique and not bleak

Is the hardest job to seek!

It requires a lot of charisma,

That's immune to any one's ukorizna. (Russian for reproach)

Many will rain

On your life's terrain!

But if you are wall-strong,

You'll be able to forestall

Any emotional intrusion

With your mentally emotional fusion!

So, be perceptive and calm

And don't let any human scum

Disturb your inner symphony

With his or her mental cacophony!

Thus, you'll be illuminated and negativity-done

And enjoy the music of the Life's Fun!

A strong body, willed by a reckless, restless, and loveless mind ends up with having ill health. Health is your wealth!

To Spread Your Spiritual Wings,

Don't Let Others Pull Your Emotional Strings!

15. Our Unification in Love is the Spiritual Stuff!

(An Inspirational Booster)

The energies of love and light
Unite us all from inside!

       A common love seat
       Is in a mutual heartbeat!

We are all One
In the God's divine plan!

       The Universal love beat
       Is also in our feet!

So, as you walk,
Try to hear the other's heart talk

       To you, to him, to Me,
       "Let Love Be;
       Let Love Be;
       Let Love Be!"

Cheating on the loved one,
You betray the inner sun,

       And your Solar System's spin
       Gets the spots of evil refill!

Being Faithful to Another is
Being True to Yourself and the Divine Father!

16. The One that is Godless is Loveless!

Live in God's Standards,

Not in Crowd's

Grandeurs!

\- - - - - - - - - - - - -

Be Kind to the Unkind;

Be One of a Kind!

\- - - - - - - - - - - - - -

Preserve Your Soul's Mold -

Love by the Moral Code!

Try to Sound Higher, Shine Brighter,

and Love Longer!

With the Umbilical Cord of Love,
We are All Connected to God from the Above!

(The Know How for <u>the Mental Dimension</u> of Soul- Resurrection)

Self-Installation

Soul's

<u>Discovery</u>

(To life-sustain, give more mental food to the brain!)

Visualize every action before taking it!

To be <u>body + spirit + mind</u> fit, be life upbeat!

Every Soul is Sojourned by this Unit of its Owner!

I Can! I Want to, and I Will!

Chaos is Ruling the World in its Every Fort,
But the Voltage of My Spirit is High and Infinite!

1. Step Three - I Am Free to Be the Best of Me!

In the Mental Dimension, featured more in my Excellence Award winning book *"Living Intelligence or the Art of Becoming!"* (*see Book Rationale*), I present the level of professional **SELF-INSTALLATION** in life. The perpetually evolving world of science and technology demands that *we develop our souls in tandem* with the exponentially growing technologically enhanced intellect and spiritual maturation.

A new Holistic Self- Concept = A New Level of Self-Consciousness!

Interestingly, *we are developing our male and female angles in a holistic unity, too,* and if any of our sides gets distorted, our tact and knowledge of the art of living that we are obtaining now will prompt *the right open-mindedness.* *So,* if your significant other prefers someone else, respect his / her choice.

Take the bad with the good; be in a wise, noble mood!

Everyone is free to operate his own lifetime and space according to his / her intelligence. Science has just started a long process of figuring out what dark energy, sizzling black holes, and a string theory can explain, and what their staggering implications are in terms of consciousness and *our souls as its carriers.* We get programmed from berth at the spiritual, cerebral, emotional, psychological, and physical levels.

However, a person can constantly study, but he remains within the limits of the basic content of his intellect. And quite rightfully, we have many educated people, but very few real intellectuals with true spiritualized souls. *So, let's elevate and illuminate each other's fate! "No soul should be left behind!"*(Edgar Cayce)

Our souls are the energy - consciousness vessels of our own space and time, and we are the ones shaping our minds and lives. The changes that we experience in life result in constant rewiring of the brain neurons. The network of their activity that is predominantly in the subconscious mode is mind-boggling, and we are rapidly transforming it if we are on the conscious evolutionary ride.

How your brain is wired determines how you are!

Because our brains are monitored by our subconscious minds, we often behave impulsively and mindlessly, *governed by the conditioned patterns of behavior* that we had accumulated in the brain - mind for years of unconscious, emotions-driven lives. However, our minds are not altogether unmanageable!

"You Better Be Unborn than Untaught!" *(Plato)*

2. Not to Ever Despair, Be More Life-Aware!

Life changes and with it, we do, too, involuntarily, continuously, and from birth. However, we do not change as separate life entities, we are changing with the entire flow of life on Earth and in the Universe.

"Nothing endures but change." (Aristotle)

The changes that we are going through now are the toughest we had ever had because humanity is *at the most remote stage of its polarity* in every aspect of life. Our medieval prejudices get in the way of our souls' progressive nobleness.

The souls are disconnected and bruised, humiliated and abused!

Thanks goodness, the process of converging of the opposites of life that we are at now has started! We have slowly, but surely come to understand an urgent necessity to unite mentally, to balance our emotional turmoil nationally and socially, and to physically preserve ourselves and the environment that we are part of. Most importantly, we have come to the revelation that *the universe is digital* and that we are an indispensable cell in its Universal Womb of Life.

We are moving on-ward, up-ward, God-ward.

What is your direction toward?

Slowly, but surely, we are changing inwardly and outwardly, becoming more inquisitive, insightful, *more body-conscious and soul-conscious*.

"The body is a visible soul; the soul is a visible soul." (Osho)

We are getting reformed in each dimension. The life twists and turns that are molding us are also changing us *physically, emotionally. mentally, spiritually and universally* if we are able to reflect on the causes of these changes and modify the consequences. We can oversee this change if we work at refining or repairing our *"Volitional I" (John Banes) consciously* and with *aware attention* to life.

The chase for the *"immediate gratification"* to get, to deceive, to self-gain remain, and *"ignorance is still the greatest enemy of the humanity!" (Albert Einstein),* but the technological revolution has unveiled new deposits of knowledge that radically change our perception of ourselves and life around us. We need *to process this knowledge in sync with emotional intelligence and spiritual enlightenment* and instill them in the young minds holistically.

Knowledge without good thinking skills destroys inner wheels!

"Life does not Adjust to Us; We Adjust to Life!"

3. The Blueprint of the Mental Soul-Enrichment

Obviously, ***there is no soul-refining without intelligence-modifying***! In the book "*Living Intelligence or the Art of Becoming*" that features the mental level in the holistic paradigm of self-creation, I introduce ***ten most essential*** **VISTAS OF INTELLIGENCE** that a soul-refining person needs to install in the brain at least at a dilettante level. At the technological age, the mind needs to be ***holistically designed***, and the expansion of knowledge at every level becomes an indispensable must for every developing soul.

Vistas of Intelligence to be installed::

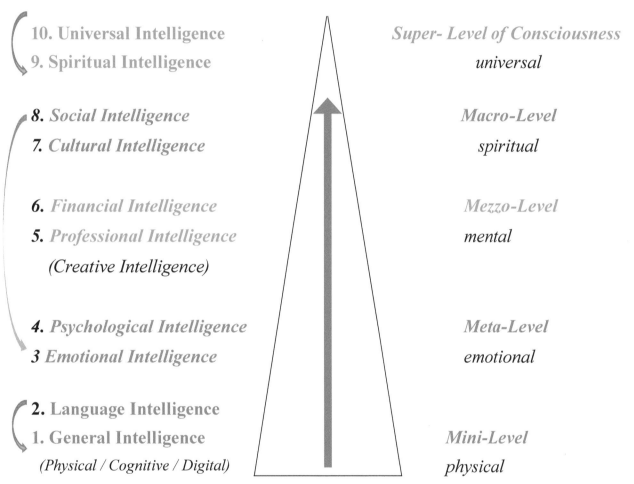

10. Universal Intelligence — Super- Level of Consciousness

9. Spiritual Intelligence — universal

8. *Social Intelligence* — *Macro-Level*

7. *Cultural Intelligence* — *spiritual*

6. *Financial Intelligence* — *Mezzo-Level*

5. *Professional Intelligence* — *mental*

(Creative Intelligence)

4. *Psychological Intelligence* — *Meta-Level*

3 *Emotional Intelligence* — *emotional*

2. Language Intelligence —

1. General Intelligence — *Mini-Level*

(Physical / Cognitive / Digital) — *physical*

Knowledge needs a lot of linking to generate Holistic Thinking!

Soul-Refining is in Mind Redesigning!

4. Disconnected Souls are Prone to Become Foes!

Regrettably, quoting Albert Einstein again, *ignorance remains to be" the worst enemy of the humanity"*, and our main goal in the mental dimension of soul-refining is to fight with ignorance in ourselves and others. It is an accepted fact that we are often driven by the automatic actions, thoughtless, media-directed behavior that disconnects our minds and hearts and makes us soul-dead. ***Disconnection is death!*** The Bible teaches us,

"The house divided against itself does not stand!"

We are becoming more ***"the race of programmed minds"*** *(David Icke)* and ***iced souls.*** great tale by *H. Ch. Anderson "Snow Queen", in which Kai got a piece of ice in the heart and Gerda had to make it melt with her love,* has a lot of implications for us. Our hearts are iced by the society's bureaucratic regulations that make us ***politically correct and impersonally driven*** to retain a job that pays the rent but depletes us of the mind + heart connection.

Therefore, many people would rather be indifferent and soul-deaf than lose the job that determines the comfort of living. The insightful, conscientious attitude to the situation that needs the heart to be involved is becoming obsolete. Our legal and educational systems are mostly infected, spreading the virus of disconnection along. Consequently, our ability to tap the vastness of the Universal Intelligence is limited by our ***intellectual laziness and stereotyped thinking.***

As a result, we grudge time needed to be spent on introspection and self-growth that wake up the soul and reestablish the lost mind + heart unity. I see this degradation in my students' souls, year in and year out, and it takes work to wake them up to self-installation transformation. But ***technology can be used to develop our intelligence, grow our consciousness, and purify the souls*** because as, science proves now, the Universal Mind is digital, and technology is a supplementary evolutionary tool in our conscious time-space relationship with the universe

Information is the mind's fruition and the soul's ammunition!

With conscious use of technology, we can stop having ***a merry-go-round life, say no to quick-fix relationships***, and put an end to an impersonal attitude to each other. We can resist the urge to use drugs and alcohol that destroy the best assets that we have – creative minds and time-limited lives.

Demystify the Know-How of Life to Thrive!

5. Mind + Heart's Unity Beats Self-Perpetuity!

Undoubtedly, to become soul-reformed, we need to be better informed! Since the Universal Mind is digital, conscious time-space relationship between our biological computers and the digital universe has become an evolutionary priority that demands putting *the mind and the heart in sync.*

The erosion of our souls, generated by their disconnection can be stopped only by those who are aware of the transformational effect of the technology on the soul and are willfully channeling the soul refinement along the path of *personal evolution that should go in a spiral way, not in a circle.*

"We all need immunity against "self-perpetuity." *(Rav. P.S. Berg.)*

Without illuminating the mind, the development of one's own self toward attaining self-knowledge and sculpturing the character, or *getting soul-enlightened*, we cannot decipher the Universal truth about life and death.

Due to high tech explosion, life has a different narrative of soul-erosion.

Conscious *self-scanning* in five dimensions of life-and auto-suggestive inspirational back-up in the *physical, emotional, mental, spiritual, and universal life dimensions* needs to be done at least once a day, before going to bed. It will help us beat self-perpetuity, raise self-awareness, and rationalize your attitude to life and living.

Eventually, as the result of the new habit of self-scanning and occasional meditation, you will be striking up friendship with new mental friends from the digital realm of the universe. The aware attention to the **body + spirit+ mind unity** will also resonate with much better health and a longer life.

"The consciousness of a man, or his immortal soul is shaped by the Informational Field of the Earth." (Dr. G. I. Shilov)

New Living Skills will come to the surface – **INTUITION** and **TELEPATHIC ABILITIES.** They will literally enable us to fly in the mind and give the soul its spiritual wings. *The ancient myth about Icarus who dared to challenge the Sun will become a reality.* I like the book *"Fly Like Icarus!"* written by a young writer *Yolanta Lensky* and addressed to children because it inspires the kids to explore the space and to stretch their minds for the solutions of new, mind-boggling ideas.

Forming the Mind, we are getting Soul-Refined!

6. The Art of Being is the Art of Becoming!

I have written in the philosophical parts of the book *(Part One and Two)* that our kids need to study **the Art of Being and Becoming** or **the Science of Life** as one of the essential subjects in school and a supplementary one in their future academic life, at its starting point

Our main action is the holistic self-construction!

In the future, <u>our intelligence will merge with artificial intelligence</u> (the *phenomenon of Singularity*), and we will be much less materialistic, more generous, caring and, of course, much more intelligent because technology will shoulder many of our worries and make a lot of problems solvable. So, only with **RATIONALIZATION** of life and conscious use of technology that feeds our thinking, can we deal with the tribulations of life calmly because they are an inseparable part of the entropy process that inevitably fluctuating between ups and downs.

The process of knowing is endless, and it is a great honor to say, like Socrates," *I know I know nothing, the rest do not know even that!"* In our quest for the meaning of the conceptual structure of life, our digitally transforming souls are learning to mentally-emotionally decipher the digital text that is transmitted to us from Above. Its connecting device is our growing intuition.

Naturally, the more mentally-emotionally-refined, informed and spiritually advanced we become, the better at self-realization we will be. The present-day market is competing for such holistically developed people. Quoting a wonderful book *"Taming the Chaos"* by Rev. Berg, we need to concentrate our will power on governing the three main aspects of "human's reformation of a soul – the mind, the heart, and the sex."

<u>Mind+ Heart + Sex must be a consciously- controlled process!</u>

These are the three beasts that we need to tame because they constitute the sacred unity of **999** and destroy the evil *666 links* of the fundamental forces of life *(Rev. Berg).* that constitute order and chaos, evolution and entropy, construction and destruction.

We know that *self-assessment and self-reflection* are the indispensable tools in such evolution of a human soul. That's why aware attention must be paid to the process of producing the outcome product - *the holistic life-awareness* that is vital in raising self-consciousness. As *Rev. P. S. Berg* puts it,

"Knowledge is the Origin of All Consciousness!"

7. The Art of Thinking is Souls-Linking!

Let us repeat again that the process of knowing the new applications of information technology is exponentially endless, and it is a great honor to say, now, like Socrates, *"The only true wisdom is in knowing you know nothing."*

In this light, our constant mental self-growth, ought to be constantly enhanced. It will prompt to us the plan of action and the degree of its urgency. Now that we are learning to emulate human thinking in a computer, new, unconditioned, holistically oriented **THINKING SKILLS** need to be developed in five levels, too. **1)** Mini - *Physical Level* **2)** Meta - *Emotional Level 3)* Mezzo - *Mental* **4)** Macro - *Spiritual 5)* Super - *Universal).*

We need to become much more skilled in the thinking field!

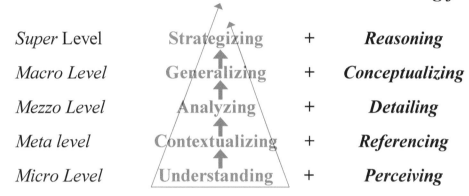

Super Level	Strategizing	+	*Reasoning*
Macro Level	Generalizing	+	*Conceptualizing*
Mezzo Level	Analyzing	+	*Detailing*
Meta level	Contextualizing	+	*Referencing*
Micro Level	Understanding	+	*Perceiving*

Mind-liberated, conceptualized reasoning and strategic thinking with much more enriched general intelligence will develop a new ability in us – *the ability to tap the Universal Informational Field* and decipher its messages that, according to *Ray Kurzweil "have a mathematical hierarchy of recognition system in our brains." Dr. R. Penrose and Dr. Hammer* are enriching our knowledge about human reasoning, stating that it has **the quantum structure** and makes up **the quantum model of consciousness**, operated by the mind's quantum parts *-microtubules.* What a mind - blowing idea!

Evidently, we should monitor our intelligence in a spiral way.

So, when the circle of the spiral gets wider, we must be going up along, leaving our limited views and society-conditioned patterns of behavior behind and cultivating new possibilities and actionable mind-sets that our digital technology exemplifies life with every day. *The process of conceptualizing of any idea* must be processed in the mind in a much more, information-enhanced, <u>conscious way of selecting new, breath-taking discoveries.</u>

"Every Time Dictates a New Frame of Mind!" *(Steve Jobs)*

8. Auto-Suggestive Inspirational Hygiene
Needs to Be on the Scene!

Our Mental Potential is
Exponential!

The mental-emotional equilibrium is
vital for the cerebrum!

So, keep consciously programming
your cells to resist the evil spells!

To life-rewind, stay in charge of
your emotions and the mind!

**Only with <u>the Conscious Mind</u> Can We Gain
What We Want to Obtain!**

9. Intelligence or Ego?

(An Inspirational Booster)

Like every human 1eing, I have a dilemma

How to separate my intelligence from the Ego "problema!"

Intelligence is light; Ego is darkness;

It dims the minds with the mob's blindness!

Intelligence is a privilege, the prerogative, and glory;

Ego is an agony and nothing, but a pure folly!

Intelligence is an open sky,

With it, you can fly!

With it, you can grow,

Expand your horizons and speed the flow!

Ego, in its turn,

Has an instant gratification form!

With it you possess;

You hurt and self-obsess!

With it, you drug or drink,

And you may even have to see a shrink!

Ego is also stagnant and stupid,

While intelligence is dynamic and lucid!

Where there's harmony, there is intelligence;

Where there's stagnation, there is ignorance!

But one should be a process, not a thing -
That's the thing!

Like taking drugs, we should admit,
You are becoming nothing, but an" IT"

Finally, we can compare life to a ladder or a hill;
You can go upward, or downward, still!

The choice is yours, and if you're not a human moth,
<u>Intelligence will always be your major driving force!</u>

"Seek and You Will Find!"

"Let him who seeks continue seeking until he finds. When he finds, he will become troubled. when he becomes troubled, he will be astonished, and he will rule over the all."

(Gospel by Judas Thomas, verse 2)

We are all in the Fort of the Almighty God!

<u>Educating yourself to be exceptional, soul-refined, and overly kind</u> is an accomplishable goal if you consciously focus on self-assessing your journey in life every day in five dimensions ***by way of X-raying your thoughts, words, feelings and action*** for their right intentions and the results that they generate in you ***physically, emotionally, mentally, spiritually, and universally.*** We need to consciously protect our soul from hyper, exaggerated reactions, sensationalism, fake soul-twisting, lying, impulsivity unwanted compromises, and random, quick -fix relationships ***Look in the mirror of your soul to make yourself whole!***

Please, Beware! The Watching Mind is Always There!

10. "Language is the Skin of the Soul!"

(Fernando Lazaro Carreter, a great Spanish linguist)

To remove your language sanity warts,

<u>*Get rid of the foul words!*</u>

Profanity breaks the soul,

And it breeds a sordid speech mole!

It gets rooted in the soul's soil,

And it steams your self-control boil!

The soil must be enriched with the mind's fertilizer,

And watered by the mouth-refined optimizer!

<u>*Then the soul will start speech sprouting*</u>

With kindness and goodness outing!

Finally, you'll grow the soul's console - garden

With your often visits into it, not sudden!

The soul's garden is your retreat,

You can be the Best of You in it!

Thus, your good speech will reform

The soul's language de-form!

And you'll be ready to proudly decree:

<u>*"My Language is Me!"*</u>

"I am responsible for what I say,

but I am not responsible for what you hear."

(Oscar Wilde)

Hold Your Tongue in the Captivity of the Mind's Run!

11. Become the Intellectual Aristocracy!

We belong to a rare class,

Found in every human mass.

        It's an intellectual aristocracy

        That has the power of mental obstinacy!

We hit ignorance at large

That holds the world in grips so much!

        The intellect of the few

        Is still very brittle in view!

The ignorance of so many

Is at the battle for a penny!

        Intelligence needs very subtle ways

        To spiritually surface!

The aristocracy of the mind

Still needs to unwind

        The hidden midst

        Of the inner width

In each one,

Fed up with the infinite fun!

        Thus, we seek a narrow way

        For a spiritual survey,

And we fill up the digital mind

With the live cells ready to unwind

        The Double Helix of an Animal DNA into

        the Five-Dimensional "Star Man's" Display!

12. Don't Assume Negative Hunches Perfume!

(An Inspirational Booster)

Try not to ever assume

Any negative hunches perfume!

> *Don't expect any trouble,*
>
> *Be immune to an unrealistic fable!*

Think big, think dreams!

Think about successful things!

> *"Like attracts Like",*
>
> *And your thoughts attract the visualized sight!*

Only if you assume the right,

Can you acquire the God's might!

> *So, to make your word right,*
>
> *Be overly bright!*

A famous saying states,

"When I am right, nobody remembers;
when I am wrong, nobody forgets."

We all make mistakes, but not all of us are able to forgive ourselves and others for them. The skill of forgiveness is the indispensable skill of self-consciousness. But as *Vladimir Vysotsky put it,*

"Only betrayals are unforgivable and trust irretrievable."

Forgiveness is a Skill that You need to Soul-Refill!

13. The Law of the Right Thinking!

The Law of the Right Thinking

Is in synch with the God's inkling;

The Law of the Right Language Use

Is in sync with the right behavior fuse!

We ignite it and often abuse

When we are emotionally defused!

Our thoughts result in words and impact our actions,

They, in turn, generate the language fractions

That damage our left brains

With bad habits refrains!

To turn them into good ones

Is impossible to be done at once!

Patience and control of a casual language muse

Are required to be used!

Tongue accuracy, corrected at a brink

Demonstrates exactly how you think!

The personal profile bricks

Are laid out by the way one speaks!

Because you and the language in you

Are the inseparable two!

So, to become a self-managing guru,

Help your emotional diplomacy come true!

Keep Your Emotions and the Tongue in the Captivity of Your Mind's Run!

14. Put the Mind and the Heart in Sync!

Feel but Think!

(An Inspirational Booster)

The mind and the heart's link

Needs to be always in synch

> *With your soul*
>
> *That must be self-consoled!*

The soul that vibrates

And kindness resonates;

> *The soul that is charged*
>
> *By a compassionate heart's surcharge;*

The soul that radiates the rays

That warm up any one's space!

> *Only such link fortifies your personal Mer-ka-bah*
>
> *And helps your soul to recover!*

<u>You are Your Brain; Be Sane!</u>

Use Technology for your Self-Ecology!

(Upload your smart phone with a new Auto-Suggestive tone!)

Harness Ignorance in the Bud; Be Overly Smart!

Soul's

<u>Recovery</u>

Verify Your Love with the Station Above!

"Take Care of the Outside for People;

Take Care of the Inside for God!"

(Robert H Schumer)

The Real Heaven in Mass is Truly in Us!

Your Goal is to Stop Being a Sleeping Soul!

To Get a Self-Creation Inkling,
Work on Your Transfromational Thinking!

1. Step Four - Being Godly in the Godless World

In the Spiritual dimension, featured in the book *"Self-Taming"* presenting the spiritual level of **SELF-REALIZATION** in the holistic paradigm of self-resurrection *(see Book Rationale).* I see soul-refining as *a spiritual battle of a godly person in a godless world.* It is our biggest challenge now! We must meet it consciously, governed by a firm faith in God, oneself, in science, and in life. Having the blueprint of soul-refining in the mind and embracing the high-tech accomplishments, we must consciously develop our *spiritualized intelligence.*

We are moving onward, upward, and God-ward!

The know-how of this movement is dramatically changing now, *helping us discriminate the fundamental notions of religiousness and spirituality.* We must put the mind into the conscious gear and channel our lives "in the **STREAM OF CONSCIOUSNESS** technique,"* when, according to a great American writer *William Falkner,* the pioneer of this method of narration in literature, we need to be in full charge of the flow of our thoughts, feelings, and actions. The conscious state of our *interior revelation* sometimes poses the question, **"To BE or Not to BE"** in the shadow of our minds.

The logic that I mention is still in the suspension

Of life's declarative review -- To Be! and No Other View!

We are at the foot of the mountain of the unknowable in neuroscience, but one thing is irreversible. Everyone tries to secure a place in the digital market, but the rules of soul-refining should never fail us on the path of performing the mission in our *technologically enhanced brutally competitive self-installation.* The qualities of human integrity must work in any situation and at any time. Unfortunately, people think in these terms only inside churches and when they pray sporadically. *But the spiritual level of self-resurrection comes after the mental one for a reason!* This is what *Sadhguru* rightfully declares,

"Being religious is following the leader; being spiritual is following the message."

Our educational and parental roles, therefore, are to instill this distinction in our children, students, staff, and the society at large. **SPIRITUALIZED SELF-CREATION** makes us better looking, more intelligent, and more confident people. No doubt, the cultivation of the mind and character is most needed now. *We cannot afford being indoctrinated; we must be true life-awareness elated!*

Spiritual Transformation is in Soul Reformation!

2. The Soul Needs Spiritual Air to Breathe!

Our souls are immortal symbiosis of **intelligence *(idea)*** and **matter *(energy)*,** and they are eternal, to begin with. <u>Intelligence and energy, or idea and matter's link govern a soul's eternal life in sync.</u>

<u>Life is a variable reality, not an absolute one!</u>

According to *the Unified Theory*, souls are not separate entities, they are part of the information field *"**the mediums"*** that connect us to the entirety of life in the universe. Every unselfish and sharing act that we commit, releases the imprisoned energy of the soul that emanates from *the Unified Field of Consciousness*, enriching it with its inner light.

Make the deposits of goodness, kindness, and love into your soul; be whole!

The discoveries by *Nassim Habamein* that I have quoted above, have a huge implication for our awareness of what life is all about, <u>fortifying the idea that we need to be more connected to the Universal Mind.</u> Meditation practices are being numerously presented online.

I consider **the Transcendental Meditation** *by Dr. John Hagelin* and **the Yoga Meditation** by the world's greatest guru *Sadhguru* to be most effective in our connection to ourselves and the Universal Consciousness that is enveloping us everywhere. Undoubtedly, the better our own unified energy of life is, the more contribution we make to *the Unified Field of Information as* **the interconnected process of energy exchange.** Truly,

"No soul is left behind!" *(Edgar Cayce)*

These beautiful words are in fact another example of a timeless auto-suggestive, ***psychologically charged mind-set*** that balances our perception of life with the help of the eternal pieces of wisdom. As a matter of fact, <u>*any verse in the Bible or any other holy book has a strong auto-suggestive spiritual effect on our souls.*</u>

According to the unifying *"String Theory"* in physics, this symbiosis is in constant vibration or fluctuations. Apparently, due to this infinite process, the life of a soul on Earth is not supposed to be stable and wholly happy. It is supposed to fluctuate between ***happy-unhappy, lucky-unlucky, sick-healthy, alive and dead***. It is based on the ups and downs of the energy flow, vibrations, a minus or plus charge, the order and chaos of life events, destruction and construction of our actions, evolution and entropy, or God and devil, governing our souls at large.

Inspiration or Desperation - that's Life's Equation!

3. Our Spiritual Volume is the Driving Force of the Evolution!

The holistic evolution of consciousness- intelligence of both the society and the world that is presented above *(Part Two)* is being now formed by an unprecedented socialization and globalization of our lives that promote our gradual consciousness ascending. The main questions everyone has to ask himself daily are: *What is the nature of my life in general?" What is the nature of my life physically, emotionally, mentally spiritually and universally wise?*

To life- devise, become holistically- wise!

We, in fact, develop *the holistic consciousness of inter-dependency* which is now working only in three-dimensions: *Hight, width, depth. I think that the evolution pushes us to its fourth dimension -* THE SPIRITUAL VOLUME that encompasses everything around us and that generates *the feeling of Oneness inside and outside of us.*

Our self-consciousness is five dimensional *(See Part Two),* and it needs to be scanned constantly from inside and outside with the help of meditation of any sort. You have a great choice on the Internet. To reconnect with my mind, I prefer *the Auto-Suggestive Meditation,* as an active impact on the soul*,* and *the Transcendental Meditation* or *the Yogi Meditation* by Sadhguru, as a passive one. The thing is, character is the main aspect, connected to the spirit that boosts our psyche, channeling us to swim against the common current of life.

Everything relates to everything. *"Our Sun is the mind that guides the solar system; the Galactic mind guides the galaxy, and the Universal mind guides the Universe, the Source of the mind that guides all creation."(David Icke)* Therefore, the process of upgrading of our conscience-intelligence needs to be viewed by us in five main philosophical levels: *Mini, Meta, Mezzo, Macro, and the Super Levels,* and such holistic self-scanning works excellently when we meditate.

Thanks to such integrity, we will see the world and ourselves in it in total connection with everything and everyone around us. At the Super Level of our self-consciousness development, we will attain *Oneness with Life,* and the state of balance will be ruling our essence, or, in other words, the time of *our Inner Renaissance* will finally come. I think that doing that we'll be helping to implement our *"Inner Engineering."* (Sadhguru)

Climb the Ladder of Intelligence to Be Done with Ignorance and Love Negligence!

4. Soul's Recovery

Any soul's recovery

Is in the Mer-ka-bah discovery! *("Flower of Life" by Drunvalo Melchizedek)*

> *The mind and heart's link*

> *Should to be in sync*

With your eternal soul

That shouldn't have any evil mole!

> *The soul that with kindness vibrates,*

> *Responds to it and resonates!*

It is always alive

With love and life!

> *Such a soul is charged*

> *By the heart's surcharge!*

It also radiates

The light rays

> *Of love and passion,*

> *Care and compassion!*

The soul's rays

Warm up the personal space

> *Around your Mer-ka-bah*

> *That deletes any emotional abracadabra!*

You become kind to the unkind;

And you behave as One of a kind!

**The Synch of the Heart and Mind will fortify your Soul
and help you Self-Console!**

5. I Do Not Faith-Trifle!

I do not faith-trifle,
I read Torah, Koran, and the Bible!

        I do it slowly, consciously,
        Seriously, and prayerfully!

These sacred books are the mines of wealth
And the rivers of our inner health!

        They divinely soul-invest
        Their holiness and life's zest!

Any sacred book, indeed,
Helps to out-power the evil seed!

        We get into the paradise of glory
        And receive the remedy against any folly!

We start to apply less eloquence
And learn to use more patience and tolerance!

        Then, the wisdom of the spiritual word
        Becomes our shield and the unbreakable sword!

With the spiritual clarity,
Life loses its primitive vanity!

        So, be consistent with the word
        Of the Holy Books that you've got!

The Love of God is the what
We reflect in Every Action and Each Thought!

        Don't Follow the Common Thought;
        Follow the Messages of God!

6. The Soul's Mildew is Everywhere in View!

The Philosophy of the Right or Wrong

hasn't undergone a Substantial Reform!

"Husbands brutalize wives, fathers abuse children, mothers make drug addicts of their fetuses, and kids who are barely teenagers commit murder in the schools." (Rav. P.S. Berg)

Being ignorant and full of folly generates bulling and soul-destroying!

Empty Talking and Praying aren't Soul -Training!

Being Impersonal makes Spiritual Maturation Reversible!

Any Religious Affiliation is not Changing the Society's Formation!

Whatever the Fight, I'll Watch from the Side!

What Do I Care for the Life's Overall Mess?
I Care Less!

7. Why Does God Test Me?

Why does God test me again and again

Without any merciful refrain?

> *How can I always smile*
>
> *If I am constantly on the trial?*

I can hardly stand after each blow

When devil pushes me, "Go down, go!"

> *If I cannot stay on the integrity path,*
>
> *I must be on trial, and not once!*

Only those who can preserve

The zero-position surf

> *Can withstand*
>
> *The wind, the storm, and the shaky sand!*

The rest must endure

The rain and a hurricane cure!

> *Until the time comes, if at all,*
>
> *When you can forestall*

The temptation whims and wants

And get on the need track bonds!

> *Only resisting the evil temptation stuff*
>
> *Can we learn to accumulate love!*

I'm Driving through the Time and Space with God on My Interface!

8. Let's Raise Our Boys as Real Men!

(An Instructional Booster)

Let's Raise Our Boys as Real Men!

Enlightened in their stem!

> *A real man is not a cloud in the pants,*
>
> *He's the one with the iron-clad guts!*

In his mental fest,

He can conquer the Everest!

> *And in his emotional out-let,*
>
> *He needs to be a real athlete,*

Able to feel, to support, to kneel,

And to sustain a marriage deal,

> *To stand tall and to forestall*
>
> *Any financial down-fall;*

To rise from ashes again and again

And to be able to rule the Carforgen!

> *His castle of love*
>
> *Is also made of strong stuff!*

His individual whims,

Regrets, doubts, and money spins

> *Should not bother him a bit*
>
> *If he wants to fit*

A rare uniform

For the best human form!

I wish every woman, at that

To find a man like that!

For the more intelligent the man,

The better woman I become!

This formula works the other way, too,

If a man wants to become a success guru!

So, let's raise our boys as real men,

Able to strengthen the human stem!

For Real Men

Are the founders of the God's Eden!

Teach them make their Soul-Work a regular Self-Talk!

"As the Parents Think, so Grows the Child"

(Rev. P.S. Berg)

Long Live the Belief in Our Kids without "IF!"

9. Christ Said to His Disciples' Net

Christ said under the disciples' hungry watch,
"On this rock, I will build my church!"

> *And so, I do,*
> *Building my church inside myself and you!*

The rock of your self-worth
Is here, on the planet Earth,

> *And your church will sit*
> *On the top of it!*

Your thoughts and feelings
Make up your congregation dealings,

> *And you are the formation*
> *Of your own obligation!*

Any church exists and prospers
Only on the bricks of the sacred Gospels!

> *So, visit your church as often as you can*
> *To prolong your spiritual life span!*

Commit to God on the porch
Of your personally built church!

> *And turn on the light in another,*
> *Without thinking, "I would rather…"*

Forgive the Unkind! Be One of a Kind!

10. Right is Our Might!

The philosophy of the right and wrong

For centuries has undergone

> *A lot of verbal bites*
>
> *And bloody religious fights!*

It was instilled in humans' race

With the birth of Christ's faith!

> *It is with His holy mission on Earth*
>
> *That we began our consciousness rebirth!*

But we theorize and downsize

His evolutionary advice!

> *We pray, we light the candles,*
>
> *But we remain vandals!*

It's so incredibly hard

To have an integrity gut

> *That's intact and has a proper digestion*
>
> *Of the truly Godward suggestion!*

There's still a lot of skepticism

About Christ's moral ascetism!

> *So, what's right and wrong*
>
> *Hasn't undergone a substantial reform!*

Religion and science

Are still in defiance

And until they reconcile their Guts,

The philosophy of the right and wrong will remain to be uguts!

(Italian for "Nonsense")

11. Our Future Being is in Soul-Refining and Self-Fulfilling!

Our intuition, like the barometer, prompts to us the right inner weather, the right thing to do, the right decision to make, or the right person to choose, but we disregard its messages.

*We often hear people say, "**I should've…, but I didn't.**" So, let's learn to trust ourselves and be more perceptive to the messages we get from the Above.*

That's the real stuff!

Soul -Training
is the Basis for Life Gaining!

There is no Self-Realization without
<u>Spiritual Transformation!</u>

In God's Mind, Every Life Story is
One of a Kind!

Auto -Induction:

I'm My Best Friend;
I'm My Beginning and My End!

12. Be a Pool of Consciousness!

Be just a pool of consciousness,

<u>Create a paradise in you,</u>

> *Accept life with all its problems,*
>
> *And enjoy it, too!*

"Be the light unto yourself",

As Buddha said,

> *For only inner freedom can create*
>
> *Your sunrise net!*

You are your own glory,

Your grandeur, and your wonder!

> *So, listen to the still voice within;*
>
> *<u>It's your inner twin!</u>*

It tells you to be calm and not afraid

Of the insecurities that are in you innate.

> *Life is insecure and complex, true,*
>
> *But it is also natural and simple, too!*

So, accept it, as such,

And cherish it very much!

> *But if you go astray in it,*
>
> *Be sure to admit it!*

A person who never does wrong, hardly ever grows.

That's how life goes!

> *A good person puts bad behind him;*
>
> *A bad person reverses this scheme!*

Lastly, be alone, not in the mob;

<u>*Be in a celibate state with your own sob!*</u>

> *Remember tomorrow will never stay;*
>
> *It's always today, as the sages say!*

Have the reins of today in your hand;

Be the master of your life's band!

> *Also, be as simple, as nature, unpretentious and deep,*
>
> *Let no one push you to a bitter steep*

Of self-guilt and imperfection,

Full of fear and self-reflection!

> *All your faults and missteps*
>
> *Are, but the defects*

That come with each product of life,

<u>*For you to improve it and thrive!*</u>

> *I love my life for its every glee;*
>
> *Let me be!*
>
> *Let me be!*
>
> *Let me be!*

Life Can't Have an Evolutionary Bet
If the Soul is Dead!

13. I Tune Myself to the Station "God!"

Protect me, God, from myself

And the other evil cells!

Protect me from sulkiness and gloominess

From silliness and mindlessness,

From despair

And lack of beware,

From the emotional dismay

And the mental decay,

From the inner hurt

And an outer exploit!

Protect me from getting on the automatic road,

Teach me to live in the conscious mode!

In my thought, I report only to God!

Auto-Induction:

God is Me; God is My Philosophy!

(The Know-How of <u>the Universal Dimension</u> of Soul-Resurrection)

Self-Salvation

The Soul's Light is <u>My Might!</u>

"Everything's shown up by being exposed to the light, and whatever is exposed to light itself becomes light."

(St. Paul)

If Light Emanates from You, Others Will Radiate It Back to You!

Make Light Your Soul's Might!

Be a Luminary, Not for Fun;
Use the Light as Your Soul's Gun!

In Our Terrestrial Life

Span,

God and We are

One!

We are All of One

Blood

In the Universal

Gut!

Don't Be Personal; Be Inter-personal!

Your Soul's Work is a Regular Self-Talk!

2. We All Go with the Universal Flow!

In our global culture,

We are all universally sculptured

      In the God's design

      By the ancestors' hands in twine!

We breathe in

Their life's cultural spin,

      We inherit their national values and illusions;

      And we suffer a lot from their blind delusions!

We feel their presence up there,

In the imperceptible somewhere!

      Their spirits are still in our hearts de facto;

      Their bodies are in the recycle bin of the matter!

The eternal battle of space and time

Is in the background of our energy twine!

      Wherever we mentally go,

      We are all in the universal flow!

I inwardly thank my parental tank

For bringing me up to life with a spank!

      I was later transformed

      Into the universally equal mob!

Due to the socially unstable fuss,

I became One with the global mass!

Being Technologically Refined,

We're Becoming More of the Artificial Mind!

3. Step Five - Self-Assess Your Life's Progress!

The Universal Dimension of life is the final one on the holistic ladder of Self-Resurrection. It is featured in the fifth book of the serial - *"Beyond the Terrestrial!"* Since all five books are holistically united, with each incorporating the previous and the next one, this book is addressing soul-refining in the *inseparable unity with the entirety of life* at each level. To get to *the Universal Level*, we need to gain better awareness of life and ourselves *(the physical level),* learn to monitor our imperfections *(the emotional level),* considerably enrich our intelligence *(the mental realm)* and live in unity with conscience and the soul *(the spiritual level).*

Being Godly in a godless world is a challenge, not a reward!

You need to stablish the auto-suggestive protection against entropic, evil energy that automatizes you. it is vital to get rid of the ruinous habit of acting on an impulse and thinking fast, without considering the implications of common thinking and society-prompted judgements.

A noble life is a life- long battle against stereotypes!

Very soon, *we'll go beyond the terrestrial boundaries up there somewhere!* Intelligence and energy, or idea and matter in synch will govern this process.

To become more life-fit, tune your soul to the Universal Life beat!

The Science of Life that is supposed to present life at large will help us prepare ourselves to new life perception. The respect for indescribable beauty and variety of life will be innate in us, and with our new knowledge, we'll become spiritually aristocratic. Doubt and fear will no longer steer!

Be doubt-aware; this devil's deadliest weapon is not for you to wear!

Our age is the age of **"SUPERHIGHWAY"***(Rav. Berg.)* It speeds our life immensely and sweeps away our previous wrong assumptions, making us reconsider the constraints of time, space, and motion. The ancient wisdom, found in sacred books, new archeologic discoveries, and mysterious happenings magnetize us even more with their sacred predictability of the future and the mesmerizing renaissance of human thought and craftsmanship. *"Those that have Eyes See, those that have Ears Hear!"*

I defeat, I conquer, I Empower with a New Digital Power!

4. God's Brain is Light at Every Sight!

(An Inspirational Booster)

God's brain is light

At every sight!

> *We are all One*
>
> *In the universal life span!*

Every galaxy and constellation

Is His formation!

> *We are unique in His brain;*
>
> *We are One in His domain!*

We do not choose to be black, yellow, or white,

Then, why do we fight?

> *Why don't we finally abstract*
>
> *From the centuries of this ignorant whack?*

Let's totally reverse

The perception of some human moths

> *And unite as one cell*
>
> *In the vast universal spell!*

If we get soul-spiritualized,

We'll become overly wise!

> *And we'll unite as One*
>
> *Under our Common Sun!*

Enlighten your Mental Main with the Knowledge of the Universal Brain!

5. Unite with the Green World Tight!

In the green world,

A tree-friend, I've got!

It's my Ispolin Tree (a giant)

That has a great power glee!

My tree is of two parts,

<u>Male and female guts.</u>

As an ancient book,

It comes from the East Ukrainian nook.

It has a huge dome of green,

And a sunny successful grin!

I pray at its side

To bring my books to their popularity sight!

I am asking the reading world

To acquire my ideas lot,

To turn the minds of millions to intelligence

<u>And delete ignorance and negligence!</u>

Then everyone could obtain

The strength to sustain

Any trouble and tribulation

With a sense of reason and elation!

Blessing myself at my Ispolin Tree,

<u>I get a powerful spiritual glee!</u>

Thus, Uniting Ourselves with the Green World, we find Balance and Emotional Support!

6. Preserve Your Inner Symphony!

(An Inspirational Booster)

Be illuminated and calm

And don't let any human scum

>*Disturb your inner symphony*

>*With his or her mental cacophony.*

Being unique and not soul-bleak

Is the hardest job to seek!

>*It requires a lot of charisma,*

>*That's immune to anyone's "criticisma"*

Many will rain

On your life's terrain!

>*But if you are wall strong.*

>*You'll be able to forestall*

Any emotional intrusion

With your mental-emotional fusion!

>*Thus, you'll be illuminated and calm*

>*And enjoy the music of the life's fun!*

To improve your life's scene, apply a lot of self-discipline!

Consciousness is the Mental-Emotional Essence of a Soul; It is the Soul Itself!

8. Your Immortal Soul Needs Conscious Control!

Be a Butterfly in Spirit;

Conquer the Four Elements of Life

with it!

Have the Self-Talk as

the Auto-Suggestive Inspirational Work!

Program your cells for

the body, spirit, and mind

resets!

It's Never too Late to choose the Self-Salvation Fate!

To Make Yourself More Life-Fit, Put on the Self-Inductive Outfit!

9. Every Morning is a Blessing!

Early morning - preparation procedure. When you wake up in the morning, don't be in a hurry to get up. Remember, your body is not a robot. It is alive, and you need to treat it as a living being consciously, giving it a chance to get back to the world of life. Harnessing the energy of the Sun on Earth, will give you access to an unlimited source of clear power. <u>Learn to program yourself in every cell for a new day and on the four elements of life that govern it.</u>

My life's steering wheel is under the Nature's spell still!

To begin with, say the mind-set above and <u>inwardly turn on the light in the body,</u> starting with the soles of your feet and finishing with picturing a bright light in the head, thus <u>waking up every cell with the morning light</u>. Then, to help the body get awake, ***start rubbing the entire body with your palms,*** intensifying the pressure and feeling how all the cells come back to life. In the belly area, rotate your palms in a cycling fashion nine times clockwise. Now, ***stretch the entire body several times and slowly get up.*** Induct yourself with:

Life is going on, and it's great in my own form!

1. Morning is the time for the ELEMENT OF WATER. Before getting into the shower, open the window in the bedroom and breathe in the fresh air of a new day. Then splash some cold water onto your face, clean your teeth in cold water, and drink a glass of water. Take a warm shower, ***inwardly reviewing your body from top to bottom with aware attention and care.*** Finish your showering with the water getting a little colder each morning until you feel quite comfortable to finish the shower with a splash of ice-cold water. It will refresh and energize the body and wake you up completely.

2. THE ELEMENT OF AIR. Your communication with air never ends, but try to breathe consciously, especially when you are outside. Start your working day with *9 deep alternate breaths* that will cleanse your left-right hemispheres and oxygenate the entire brain. To do that, <u>close your right nostril with a thumb and breathe in through the left nostril</u>. Then, close the left nostril with your forefinger, opening the right nostril and breathe out through it. Alternate your breaths in this fashion. *Men should start breathing in through the right nostril.* **<u>Breathe in</u>** health, love, success; **<u>breathe out</u>** <u>sickness, indifference, failure, etc</u>. You can do the alternate breathing with any of the mind-sets in this book, breathing in the first part of it and breathing out the second one.

Inspiration or Desperation is My Life's Equation!

10. Enlighten Your Being with a Better Soul- Feeling!

3. THE ELEMENT OF FIRE. a) The time of the power of fire comes at noon, and we need <u>to fuel up our cells with the Sun rays</u>. To warm up your cells, breathe them in and out *21 times*. Doing that, look at the Sun, a lamp, a candle, or, on a rainy day, just picture the Sun and your being warmed up by its energizing touch. Start doing ***alternative breathing of the sun rays*** through your nose. Breathe in the sun rays, inducting health, breathe out sickness, love vs. hatred, success vs. failure, piece vs. discord, etc. Burn them all out ***with the determination*** of ***your inner flame formation.***

My sickness is burnt in the violet fire of my life's desire!

b) Looking at the Sun, ***do some breathing of the Sun rays with your eyes***. Start breathing in through your left eye, closing the right one with a palm for a few second and breathe out through the right eye. Do the same breathing in the opposite direction<u>. The two electrical currents (*in-out*)</u> that you enact while such breathing, ***get electrified, filling up your body's electrical station with energy*** that determines your living during the day. If you feel uncomfortable doing that when other people might be watching, remember a very good proverb:

Dogs are barking, but the caravan is walking!

4. THE ELEMENT OF EARTH a*)* After 6 pm, when the Sun goes down, the Element of Earth comes to power. It brings us down to earth, calms us down, and prepares us for the night trip into the universal realm. Take a quick warm shower. Stepping out of the bathtub, <u>shake off your body in the same fashion a dog does,</u> coming out of water. All the problem out; ***let the earth process them into something better***. Be thankful to the Earth for grounding them down and freeing you of them. Induct yourself with the attitude of gratitude.

<u>Thank you, dear God, for Your Everlasting Support!</u>

b) Before going to bed, get totally undressed and lie down, ***letting your body breathe in and out the cool of the coming night*** in a very relaxed manner for a few minutes. Reflect on what good you have done during the day, thanking God for His support and asking for assistance with whatever comes / came your way. Don't worry, ***any Gordian knot will be cut***! Get under a warm blanket and ***turn off the inner light, in the opposite direction, from the head to the feet,*** gradually, consciously, and gratefully.

Sleep Tight and Accumulate Your Soul's Might!

11. Program the Soul for Every Day's Boost and Console!

Just for today,

Live though the day,

       Without tackling in advance

       All my problems at once!

Just for today,

Be happy per say!

       Even if it doesn't feel like luck,

       Be happy just for the fact!

Just for today, be emotionally perky

In your my mind and while working,

       For mental loafing

       Pushes you to a harmful doping!

Just for today, widen up your soul

To be kind to someone in need of console,

       But do it without being found,

       For such announcing doesn't count!

Just for today, do two things at least

That you like to do the least!

       Thus, you'll exercise

       Your will power enterprise!

Just for today, don't show your hurt feelings

By someone's unkind dealings!

Nor get upset or worried,

Let the other party be consciously sorry!

Just for today, be very agreeable

Even to something totally unforeseeable,

For who can ever predict

The Mighty God's verdict?

Just for today, look beautiful and be dressed becomingly,

To feel special and unique overwhelmingly,

For being common, or having bad manners

Doesn't grant you the God's wonders!

Just for today, put the two pests,

Hurry and indecision at rest!

For being doubtful

Makes you less powerful!

Just for today, have a quiet half hour

To regain my reserve and will-power!

Thus, you'll heal the anxieties of a broken heart

And charge anew your best-shot gut!

Just for today, don't fret

Anything that's fear- bereft,

For any unreasonable fright

Depletes you of the unbeatable might

That charges your personal magnetism

With its unique optimism!

Just for today, put a smile on my face

And let your personality surface!

Just for today, accept your life, as such,

But appreciate it twice, as much,

For as you give to the world,

So does the world give to thee,

Thus, you could finally say,

"I am proud of Me!"

Self-Induction:

My Evil-Immune Soul Needs Conscious Control!

"Be conscious. Consciousness mobilizes!"

(Neale Donald Walsch – "Conversations with God)"

"We are What we Repeatedly Do.

Excellence is, therefore, not an Act, It's a Habit!"

(Aristotle)

12. I'm Faithful to My Soul!

To be faithful to my soul,

I learn self-sufficiency and self-console!

        I consult my internal gut

        And talk to it, without any but!

But how to keep my mouth shut

When the enemy spills out her / his gut?

        How to remain calm

        And listen quietly to his / her angry scum?

The inner depth of me

Revolts against that hateful glee!

        I cannot display my other cheek to it

        For him / her to strike it without a remit!

My soul's gut responds with the provision,

"Just calmly install in him / her the vision

        Of the soul's deteriorating health

        That pushes forward his / her untimely death!

Then the side of the cheek wouldn't matter

Because his / her soul might be in the gutter!"

        So, for anger to subside,

        Don't try to be overly right!

Remember that we radiate

What our souls emanate!

Calm Down Your Inner Storm with a warm "Shalom!"

13. Choosing Light

(An Inspirational Booster)

<u>The Bible teaches, "Choose light!"</u>

For happiness is at your side!

> *Choosing life, you choose joy,*
>
> *And you learn to life-enjoy!*

Choosing sadness,

You kill your gladness!

> *Trying to always choose smiley emotional food,*
>
> *You put yourself in a good mood,*

But choosing a serious self-reflection,

You clad yourself in doom and frustration!

> *Only choosing light and life,*
>
> *<u>Do we manage to be alive!</u>*

"You Can Be Light, or You Can Be Darkness,

<u>But You Cannot Be Both!"</u>

(Elinor Roosevelt)

Like the Radiant Sun, Be a Shiny One!

14. On the Beam of Light

(An Inspirational Booster)

Like Einstein, I travel on the beam of

Light,

When I am down and blue in-

side!

I send myself up to the cosmic

Space

To demagnetize my toxic mental

Base!

I remove there my spiritual size

Ban

And lengthen up my lifetime

Span!

Thus, I energize my batteries

Anew

And come back to earth

Like new!

Everything I Do, I Have, I See Gladdens Me!

Self-Induction:

I'm driving through the Time and Space
with Faith *(Love, Success, Health)* on My Interface!

15. My Soul's Mantra

Light is My Psychic Protection, My Law, and the Soul's Reflection! The Light in Me is All You Should See!

"God is the celestial light that we learn to process."

(Rav. P. S. Berg)

Auto-Induction:

Luminosity is My Soul's Intellectually Spiritualized Velocity!

Soul's

Resurrection

Assess Your Self-Progress – Assess!

The Fractals of Intellectually Spiritualized Beings:

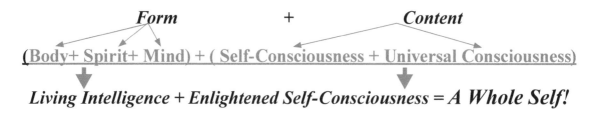

Form + *Content*

(Body+ Spirit+ Mind) + (Self-Consciousness + Universal Consciousness)

Living Intelligence + Enlightened Self-Consciousness = A Whole Self!

Soul-Resurrection is My Own Self-Reflection!

Create Your Own Your Time - Space Paradise!

Climb the Ladder of Spiritualized Intelligence to Be Done with Ignorance and Life Negligence!

1. My Soul is the Perpetua Mobile!

I do not need to justify myself;

I know who I am in my every cell!

IF my spirit is not broken,

I can physically be

Re-woken!

I am spiritually re-woken

if my spirit is

Not broken!

"If you want to come to Me, deny yourself!"

("The Words of Christ, 1979)

Auto-induction:

I Connect My Mind and the Heart in One Beat!

I Am Life -Up-Beat!

2. The Aristocracy of the Soul is Our Ultimate Goal!

To sum up, soul-refining and self-modification begin when we start paying more attention to our bodies and our inner enrichment. The state of self -reflection is of major importance here. We are driven by evolution and entropy, order and chaos. A man creates himself by way of getting rid of chaos in his soul and putting his life in order. Only by sorting out self-growth accomplishments and destroying the entropy of bad habits, can we *synthesize the heart and the mind 's beat* = **THE FUNDAMENTAL ACT OF SELF-PERFECTION.** If a person generates order in his mind consciously, he creates *order in his cells and in the entire Informational Field of the body*. Order heals, calms us down, helps us think rationally, and, it teaches our souls the basics of *Emotional Diplomacy.*

At the end of the tether, order regulates the inner weather!

Obviously, chaos and destruction are evil. But we cannot eliminate evil altogether because it is part of the divine plan that constitutes unity by creating polarity. *It is the balance between the two opposites* that we should be seeking, starting with self-knowledge and following the lead of the Universal Mind, or God. There are a few essential features that people of **SOUL-ARISTOCRACY** and inner **NOBILITY** should display:

1. rationality, self-confidence, a noble display of intellect;

2. reserve, self-control, composure. *No display of emotions in public – a calm mask on the face. a respectful attitude;*

3. introspection, discipline, and self-restriction;

4. no loud laughing, yelling, noble reverence for the elders;

5. dignity in the eyes, good manners, an erect posture;

6. a slightly - noticeable smile on the face;

7. slow, calm, low -voiced speaking and a kind interest in interaction with anybody;

8. self-respect, self-sufficiency, and self-reliance.

Self-Reflection is a Progressive Discovery of Self-Imperfection!

3. I Don't Live Automatically or Statically!

I don't live automatically,

Commonly, or statically,

> *Nor do I live sporadically,*
>
> *And too emphatically!*

I live continuously

<u>*And consciously!*</u>

> *My immortal soul*
>
> *Needs a conscious control!*

It follows the lead of my thought

And then communicates it to the emotional fort.

> <u>*My soul talks to me through intuition*</u>
>
> *And protects me against the spirit's depletion!*

If I live thoughtfully and dynamically,

My life changes dramatically!

> *I program myself on the pulse,*
>
> *Happy, happy, happy, thus,*

And I never reverse it into,

Snappy, snappy, snappy fuss!

> *Only with light in my inner sight,*
>
> *Can I be full of unbeatable might!*

So, defy the gravity of a common thought,

<u>*And be aboard with the Almighty God!*</u>

Only in Such Unity Can We Gain Spiritual Maturity!

4. Have a Meditative Fest! Be the Best!

(An Inspirational Booster)

Have a meditative fest,

Take the common God's test!

Relax your body, mind, and spirit

Without any doubt in this action's merit!

Fill yourself up in the Universal Energy Field

That is full of life's benefit!

It flows in and Out

For you to sprout

The shoots of connection

Between the bod, the spirit, and the mind in reflection!

"Self-Consciousness is the product of self-creation!"

(Carl Yung)

"My tastes are simple. I can easily be satisfied with the best"

(Winston Churchill)

"Ease is a greater threat to progress than hardship!"

(Denzel Washington)

Personal Discipline and Stability Connect Us to the Infinity!

5. I Am a Free Thinker!

I Say "Adieu!" to My Endless
Life's Ado!

I am Not Indoctrinated;
I am Self-Liberated!

I Burn the Negative Crap
Off My Mind and the Lap!

I don't Assume Anything Wrong.
I'm Godly Strong!

Use technology for your Soul-Ecology!

"The Greatest Creation of Man is He Himself!"
(Michael Angelo)

6. I Run My Own Soul!

(Inspirational Boosters)

I run my own soul;

I Self-Console!

I don't let anybody

To run my mind or the body!

No one is in charge

Of my life that much!

"Let God and let go!"

Is the motto of my personal show!

Only the Almighty God

Can tell me what

I should, or shouldn't do

In my personal life's ado!

"The light of the body is the eye. If, therefore, the eye be kind, the whole body shall be full of light, but if the eye be evil, the whole body shall be full of darkness."

(The Words of Christ)

Every bruisedsSoul needs to be Self-Governed and Self-Consoled!

Auto-Induction:

In My Thought, I Report Only to God!

7. I'm a Woman / Man-Ispolin!

(An Inspirational Booster)

I'm a woman / man-Ispolin; *(a Spiritual Giant in Russian)*

<u>I'm both masculine and feminine</u>!

I declare the priority

Of my soul's immunity!

With its width, I encompass

The stars, the galaxies, and the universes in a mass!

The energy of life and the entropy of death

Are in the orderly chaotic mess!

But I try to preserve

My inner soul's surf,

And I continue to admire

<u>My life's satire!</u>

In it, gladness and sadness

Are interwoven with the Universal Oneness

To make us appreciate, thus,

The life's happiness farce!

- -

We do not choose to be white, yellow or black, gay or straight!

<u>That's the choice of your fate!</u>

Your Life's Equation lies in the Spiritual Invasion!

8. Cleanse Your Soul of the Old Stuff,

And Give the World the Best You Have!

(An Inspirational Booster)

To give the world the best you have,

<u>Upload the will and spiritual stuff!</u>

No anger, no fear;

No attitude, no love smear!

No hurry, no haste

No worry, no waste!

Just have a lot of zest

To give the world your very best!

Live consciously and without a frown

<u>To slow up your slow down!</u>

Expand your soul's enterprise and become overly wise!

"Those who don't learn from the past

are doomed to repeat it!"

(Ancient wisdom)

Self-Induction:

In My Soul's Quest, I Manifest My Best!

9. I Infuse My Self-Realization Fuse!

(Soul -Assessment)

Every day, when you are without any soul's mask,

I address myself and ask,

> *"What have I done today*

> *For my physical array?*

Have I added a bit

To my emotional up-beat?

> *Have I enriched*

> *My mental out-reach?*

And on the spiritual plane,

Have I gotten closer to God's domain?"

> *Finally, thinking universally,*

> *What's your contribution to life irreversibly?*

So, don't waste your daily soul's zest

To just possess

> *Use it to infuse*

> *Your Self-Realization fuse!*

"Your Life is Your Making!" *(Sadhguru)*

10. In My Thought, I Live Upward!

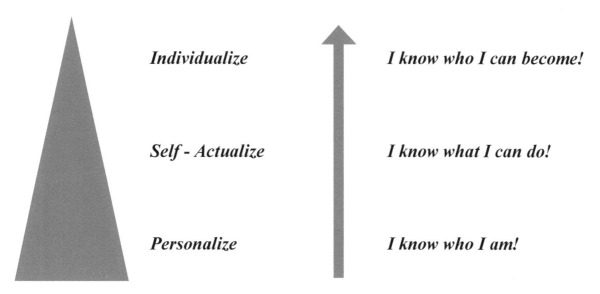

Individualize	I know who I can become!
Self - Actualize	I know what I can do!
Personalize	I know who I am!

I Don't Live Downward!

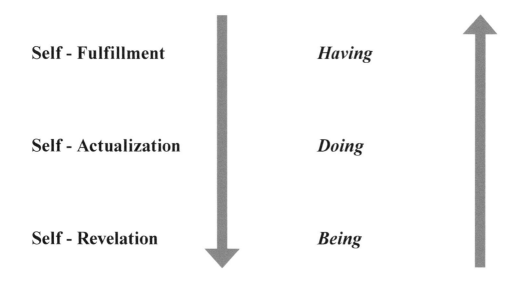

Self - Fulfillment	Having
Self - Actualization	Doing
Self - Revelation	Being

I Live Upward!

Everyone is the total of his thoughts and words! I am uplifting mine to never be lost in the life's twine!

God, the Sky, and the Earth constitute Your Self -Worth!

Post Word

"A Happy Man is a Wise Man!"
(The Mayan Wisdom)

I Glamorize
My Soul
To Be Spiritually
Whole!

I Make my heart smart and the mind kind;

I connect them with the Godly Soul's Wind!

I keep my noble soul intact, and I seal it up

against any evil act!

I'm Never at Rest; I Am on a Spiritual Quest!

The Soul's Eye through the Ear of Rye!

"We Have Two Eyes –
The Earthly Eye and the Spiritual One."

(Nikola. Tesla)

I Live with Elation;
I am the Person with
A Strong Spiritual
Foundation!

I Never Whine;
I Soul-Shine!

I Can Roam Any Terrains with a Refined Soul in My Veins!

2. The Soul's Ammunition is in Mission!

The chart below will help you beautify your everyday life a little more thoughtfully and consciously with some astrological information. *Your daily plan of action will have some spiritualized outlay.*

Days of the Week	Planets	Meaning	Colors
1. Sunday	*The Sun*	*Mercy*	*yellow*
2. Monday	*The Moon*	*Judgement*	*white*
3 Tuesday	*Mars*	*Beauty*	*red*
4. Wednesday	*Mercury*	*Victory*	*green*
5. Thursday	*Jupiter*	*Glory*	*blue*
6. Friday	*Venus*	*Foundation*	*violet*
7 Saturday	*Plato*	*A New Beginning*	*black*

Your soul-refining is being done in *the physical, emotional, mental, spiritual, and universal realms.* It is an integral process that never ends. Have the holistic paradigm of self-creation at the front of your mind to guide yourself by it, and **do soul-refining** daily to reject, resist, and reform any deform..

I'm on the Holistic Paradigm of My Soul-Refining!

Super level	**Super-Consciousness**	*Self-Salvation*
Macro level	**Self-Consciousness**	*Self-Realization*
Mezzo level	**Mind**	*Self-Installation*
Meta level	**Spirit**	*Self-Monitoring*
Mini level	**Body**	*Self- Awareness*

Body+ Spirit+ Mind + Self-Consciousness+ Universal Consciousness!

The Synergy of Every Soul's Spiritual Gain Helps Us Evil- Sustain!

I Ovulate, I Generate, I Create, and I Consecrate My Soul's Fate!

With Grace Inside, I Am Full of Spiritual Might!

Dr. Ray with Her Inspirational Say:

1. *"**Emotional Diplomacy** or **Follow the Bliss of the Uncatchable Is!**"/ **Editorial** LEIRIS, New York, USA,2010*

2. *"**Four Dimensions of a Soul**" (Auto-Suggestive Psychology in Russian) / LEIRIS Publishing, New York, USA,2011*

3. *"**Americanize Your Language, Emotionalize Your Speech!**" / Nova Press, USA, 2011*

4. *"**It Too Shall Pass!**" (Inspirational Boosters in Four Dimensions) / Xlibris, 2012*

5. *"**I am Strong in My Spirit!**" (Inspirational Boosters in Russian) / Xlibris, 2013.*

6. *"**Language Intelligence or Universal English**" (Method of the Right Language Behavior), **Book One** /Xlibris, 2013 - Also, Stonewallpress,2019*

7. *"**Language Intelligence or Universal English**" (Remedy Your Language Habits," **Book Two** /Xlibris, 2013 – Also, Stonewallpress,2019*

8. *"**Language Intelligence or Universal English,**" (Remedy Your Speech Skills) **Book Three** /Xlibris, 2013- Also, Stonewallpress,2019*

9. *"**My Solar System,**" (Auto-Suggestive Psychology for Inner Ecology) Xlibris, 2015*

Books on Self-Resurrection:

10. *"**I Am Free to Be the Best of Me!**"- (Physical Dimension) - Toplinkpublishing.com. Sept. 2017) – Second Edition, Book Whip, 2019*

11. *"**Soul-Refining!** (Emotional Dimension) (Toplinkpublishing.com. May 2017) - Second Edition, Book Whip, 2019*

12. *"**Living Intelligence or the Art of Becoming**" (Mental Dimension)- (A New Paradigm of Self-Creation) Xlibris, 2015 - Second Edition, Bookwhip,2019*

13. *"**Self-Taming**" (Spiritual Dimension)- Book Whip, 2019*

14. *"**Beyond the Terrestrial!**"!) - (Universal Dimension) Xlibris, June 2016- / Second Edition -, Book Whip, 2019 15 /" Third Edition - URLink Print and Media, 2019*

16. *"**The State of Love from the Above!**"- Book Whip, 2019 / "Love Ecology"- Second edition- Prime Solutions / 2020.*

17. *"**Self-Worth**"- Parchment /2020*

www. language – fitness.com / Emotional Diplomacy.com

- rimma143@hotmail.com / Tel. (203) 212-2673

The pictures and designs are by **Yolanta Lensky** Yolantalensky1979@gmail.com

To Become More Life Fit

Tune Your Soul to the Universal Life's Beat!

Don't Be Life-Beaten,

Don't be Life-Smitten;

Don't be Life-Paralyzed -

Be Life-Mesmerized!

"A Happy Man is a Wise Man!

(The Mayan Wisdom)